Simple Home Cooking

Cake Decorating

Publisher's Note: Raw or semi-cooked eggs should not be consumed by babies, toddlers, pregnant or breastfeeding women, the elderly or those suffering from a chronic illness.

Publisher & Creative Director: Nick Wells
Project Editor: Laura Bulbeck
Art Director: Mike Spender
Layout Design: Jane Ashley
Proofreader: Kathy Steer
Special thanks to Emma Chafer and Esme Chapman

For all cake decorating supplies by mail order:
Squires Kitchen, The Grange, Hones Yard, Farnham, Surrey, GU9 8BB.
Tel: 0845 61 71 810 Mail: customer@squires-shop.com
For bakeware and paper cases by mail order:
Lakeland, Alexandria Buildings, Windermere, Cumbria, LA23 1BQ.
Tel: 01539 488 100. www.lakeland.co.uk

This is a **FLAME TREE** Book

FLAME TREE PUBLISHING
Crabtree Hall, Crabtree Lane
Fulham, London SW6 6TY
United Kingdom
www.flametreepublishing.com

First published 2013

A copy of the CIP data for this book is available from the British Library.

All images © Flame Tree Publishing Ltd, except for the following which are © **Shutterstock.com** and the following contributors: front cover Duard van der Westhuizen; 4 & 68 Rose-Marie Henriksson; 9 Sea Wave; 11 Gayvoronskaya_Yana; 14b & 182 Eric Limon; 15t & 112 Photocrea; 16 M. Unal Ozmen; 20b Natalia Bratslavsky; 21t tale; 23t iva; 31 ffolas; 41 & 208 Pete Pahham; 43 & 122 Mariya Volik; 47 & 180 Andre Blais; 49 & 142 Jack Z Young; 51 & 82 Mircea BEZERGHEANU; 57 & 158 Dan Kosmayer; 59 & 184 Karen H. Ilagan; 60 cristi180884; 63t & 136 tratong; 66b & 190 oksix; 70, 98, 124 Hannamariah; 76 ygor; 78 nick vangopoulos; 86 vseb; 92 MARCELODLT; 94 Mariya Volik; 102 Alex Hubenov; 104 Prezoom.nl; 110 Dulce Rubia; 114 Mihai Simonia; 116 Shane Maritch; 118 BestPhotoStudio; 132 Andy Lim; 134 Ksju; 138 Karen Grigoryan; 140 Robert HM Voors; 144 Yeko Photo Studio; 150 Gordana Sermek; 154 Vania Georgieva; 156 Prezoom.nl; 160 Szasz-Fabian Ilka Erika; 162, 202, 216 John Kroetch; 166 SmudgeChris; 168 jokerpro; 170 Ksju; 172 Hank Shiffman; 176 ZeteoPhoto; 178 janecat; 188 RexRover; 192, 246 Ruth Black; 204 apolonia; 210, 224 Vania Georgieva; 220 Andrea Slatter; 222 Simone van den Berg; 226, 238 Andrea Slatter; 228 Monkey Business Images; 230 Peter Baxter; 232 Cristian Kerekes; and © **Getty Images** and the following: 39 & 126 Michael Powell; 74 Anna Williams; 90 James Baigrie/FoodPix; 100 Paul Austring; 130 Michael Powell; 240 Torie Jayne; and © **StockFood** and the following: 96 Garlick, Ian; 194 Food Image Source/Michael Skarsten; and © **iStockphoto** and the following: 80 PaulaConnelly; 88 Eddisonphotos; 146 MCCAI; 186 sbossert; 200 starfotograf; 212 MorePixels; 218 LaureniFochetto; 236 Vesivus; 244 zennie.

Simple Home Cooking

Cake Decorating

**FLAME TREE
PUBLISHING**

Contents

Cake
Basics

There is nothing better than the smell of homemade cake, especially one that you have baked and decorated yourself. Essential equipment and key ingredients as well as basic techniques and recipes will help you enormously in your quest to create the perfect base for your specially designed cakes. Whether as an accompaniment to afternoon tea or as the centrepiece to a dinner party, there is no occasion that doesn't call for a slice of cake!

Ingredients

*

In baking, most cakes are made by mixing sugar, fats, flour and eggs together. During the mixing, air is incorporated into the mixture to greater or lesser degrees to make it rise during baking. As a cake mixture bakes, the strands of gluten in the flour are stretched and the heat hardens them to give a light sponge-like texture.

Sugar

Sugar is not just included to give sweetness to cakes, it also produces a structure and texture that make a cake tender, so always choose the correct type for your recipe.

- Granulated Sugar – This is the standard sugar that you add to your tea. It comes in white and golden unrefined varieties and is used for toppings. The coarseness of granulated sugar means that it does not dissolve easily and is not designed for most baking recipes, so is no good for the creaming method.

- Caster Sugar – This is a fine-ground granulated sugar, which also comes in white and golden (or 'natural') unrefined varieties. It blends easily with butter and margarine when beaten or 'creamed' into light sponge mixtures.

- Soft Light and Dark Brown Sugars – These cream well and are usually used in richer cakes or spicy fruit mixtures such as carrot cake, and in recipes where rich colour and flavour are needed.

Store this sugar in a tightly sealed container to prevent it from drying out. If it does become dry or lumpy, pound it back into crystals with the flat end of a rolling pin before you use it.

∾ Muscovado Sugar – This sugar is natural and unrefined, with a deep brown colour and rich flavour that makes fruit cakes extra special. It comes in light and dark varieties.

Eggs

∾ Storing – Always store eggs in the refrigerator, but remove them an hour or so before you start to bake, as better results will be achieved if you allow them to reach room temperature before using. This is because, at this temperature, eggs will whisk better and achieve more aeration.

This not only gives more volume to the mixture, but also allows the eggs to blend in more easily. Cold eggs used straight from the refrigerator can curdle or split a mixture.

∾ Egg Types – Eggs sold as 'value' or 'economy' can be used for baking cakes and cupcakes, particularly if you are working to a budget (but do not forget the welfare issues involved in this choice). Also, do remember that these may be ungraded and of different sizes, so, for best results, buy eggs marked as 'medium' and 'large'. If you do use economy eggs, make sure to note the sizes you are using and try to even out the quantity by, say, using 1 large and 2 small eggs instead of 3 medium-sized ones.

Ingredients

~ **Egg Powder** – Dried egg-white powder gives good results and can be substituted in royal icing recipes, or in recipes where you are unsure about using raw egg whites in the case of pregnant women, the very young or the elderly.

Flours

Plain white flour provides the structure of a cake, but contains nothing to make a cake rise, so cakes that do not need raising agents are made with plain flour. Most recipes using plain flour have bicarbonate of soda or baking powder added to them to make the cakes rise. It is always advisable to sift this into the mixture to incorporate the raising agents evenly.

~ **Self-raising Flour** – This has raising agents already added, that will add air to make a cake rise, so is used for light sponge mixtures.

If you have only plain flour available, add 2¹/₂ tsp baking powder to 225 g/8 oz plain flour to make it into a self-raising flour.

~ **Storing Flour** – White flours should be stored in a cool dry place for up to six months, but wholemeal flours will not keep as long, as they have a higher fat content. So check the use-by date on all packs. Flour is best stored in a sealed airtight container. Always wash and dry this thoroughly before refilling and never add new flour to old. Small micro-organisms will form in very old flour, from the protein, and these can be seen as tiny black specks that will spread into new flour. If you do not have a container, store the opened paper bag inside a large plastic bag and make sure all flour is kept dry. Damp flour weighs more and therefore alters the recipe, which could lead to heavy or flat cakes.

Raising Agents

Raising agents are added to flour to make cakes rise and produce a light texture. It is important to be accurate when measuring these fine powders out, so always use a measuring spoon.

~ **Baking Powder** – This is a mixture of bicarbonate of soda and cream of tartar. When liquid is added, the powder fizzes and bubbles and produces carbon dioxide, which expands with heat during baking and gives an airy texture. Be careful not to use very hot or boiling liquid in mixtures, as these can reduce the power of baking powder.

~ **Bicarbonate of Soda or Baking Soda** – This is a gentler raising agent and is often used to give melted or spicy mixtures a lift. Cakes will have a bitter flavour if too much is added, so measure this out carefully and accurately with a proper measuring spoon, not a domestic teaspoon.

Fats

Fat adds structure, texture and flavour to cakes and improves their keeping qualities. Always remove them from the refrigerator before using them – they are much easier to mix in when at room temperature.

~ **Butter and Hard Block Margarine** – Butter and hard margarine can be interchanged in a recipe, and the results will be the same. Butter, however, will always give a better flavour to cakes and so, if they are for a special occasion, is it well worth spending a little extra on this.

Ingredients

❧ Soft Margarine – Sold in tubs, this is wonderful for using in all-in-one sponge recipes where all the ingredients are quickly mixed together in one bowl. This fat always produces good results and is quick and easy to use because it does not have to be used at room temperature but can be taken straight from the refrigerator. Do not substitute soft margarine for butter or hard block margarine in a recipe, as it is a totally different kind of fat, which will not produce the same results. Cakes using soft margarine usually require extra raising agent, so do follow the recipe carefully and do not be tempted to over-beat the mixture, as it will become wet and the cakes may sink. Up to 2 minutes of whisking with an electric mixer is fine to make a smooth mixture.

Dried Fruits

❧ Dried Vine Fruits – Fruits such as raisins, currants, sultanas and cranberries are usually sold ready-washed and prepared for baking, but it is still worth looking through them for pieces of stalk and grit before baking. Dried cranberries, sometimes sold as 'craisins', add a sweet, fresh flavour to cakes, similar to dried cherries. As they are bright red in colour, these can be used as a topping or decoration, as well as baked into mixtures. Fresh cranberries also make a colourful cake decoration.

❧ Glacé Cherries – Sold thinly coated in syrup, these come in a dark maroon natural colour and a brighter red colour, the latter usually being cheaper than the natural variety. These cherries keep well stored in their tubs in a cool place. Always wash the syrup off the cherries before baking, as it will cause the cherries to sink in the mixture.

❧ Citrus Peels – Bright and colourful, these add a zesty tang to recipes. Dried orange, lemon and lime peels can be bought as whole large pieces in syrup or a sugar glaze, or ready chopped into small pieces coated in light syrup in a tub (often sold as 'mixed peel'). Keep both varieties in a cool place to prevent crystallisation or drying out of the fruit.

~ Dried Apricots – Dried apricots are a great addition to fruit cakes and are richer and sweeter than the fresh fruits. Some dried apricots are shrivelled and have a dark brown colour and these need soaking before use. Look for packs of the ready-to-eat varieties, which are soft and moist and ready to use for baking. Organic dried apricots usually have a brighter orange colour and a better flavour, so are worth looking out for.

Spice

Most dried spices have a reasonably long shelf life but will not keep indefinitely, and remember that they will gradually lose their aroma and flavour. It is a good idea to buy in small quantities only when you need them. You will find that both light and heat affect the power and flavour of spices, so, if stored in clear glass jars, keep them out of the light – the best place to store spices is in a dark, cool, dry place.

Flavourings

Flavouring extracts are very concentrated and usually sold in liquid form in small bottles (*see* right). For example,a teaspoon measure will usually be enough to flavour a cake mixture for 12 cupcakes.

　Ingredients

Vanilla and almond extracts are ideal to impart their delicate flavours into cake mixtures and you will find the more expensive extracts give a finer and more natural flavour. Rosewater can be used for flavouring both cake mixtures and icings and has a delicate, perfumed flavour. Fruit flavourings, such as lemon, lime, orange and raspberry, will give a fresh twist to mixtures and icings.

Chocolate

Indulgent chocolate is a useful ingredient for any cake decorator, whether used just to make the cake itself or as a delicious icing too. For the best results and a professional finish and flavour, it is always advisable to buy the highest quality chocolate you can find, although this will be more expensive. Better quality chocolates contain a higher percentage of real cocoa fat, which gives a flavour and texture far superior to cheaper varieties.

Cheaper chocolate labelled as 'cooking' or 'baking' chocolate contains a much smaller percentage of cocoa solids and is best avoided in favour of better-quality eating chocolate.

The amount of cocoa fat or solids contained in chocolate will be marked on the wrapper of any good-quality chocolate. Those marked as 70 per cent cocoa solids will give the best results and you will find that this chocolate is shiny and brittle and it should snap very easily.

- **Dark Chocolate** – Also known as 'plain' or 'plain dark' chocolate, this is the most useful all-purpose type of chocolate for baking, as it has a good strong flavour.

- **Milk Chocolate** – Milk chocolate has sugar added and is sweeter than dark, so is also good for melting for icings and decorations.

- **White Chocolate** – This is not strictly chocolate, as it contains only cocoa butter, milk and sugar. It is expensive and the most difficult to work with, so must be used with care. It is best to grate it finely and keep the temperature very low when melting it.

- **Chocolate Cake Covering** – This is a cheaper substitute, which contains a minimum of 2.5 per cent cocoa solids and vegetable oil. It is considerably cheaper than real chocolate and the flavour is not so good, but it is easy to melt and sets quickly and well for a coating.

- **Cocoa Powder** – Cocoa powder needs to be cooked to release the full flavour, so blend it with boiling water to make into a paste, then cool, before adding to a recipe, or sift it into the bowl with the flour.

- **Drinking Chocolate** – Be aware that this is not the same as cocoa, as it contains milk powder and sugar. Some recipes may specify using drinking chocolate and these are successful, but do not substitute it for cocoa powder, as it will spoil the flavour of a cake.

Ingredients

Key Equipment

Bakeware

It is worth investing in a selection of high-quality tins, which, if looked after properly, should last for many years. Choose heavy-duty metal tins that will not buckle or the new flexible silicone tins – these are easy to turn out, most need very little greasing and they also wash and dry easily.

∾ **Deep Cake Tins** – With deep cake tins, you can buy both round or square tins, depending on preference. They vary in size from 12.5–35.5 cm/5–14 inches with a depth of between 12.5–15 cm/5–6 inches. A deep cake tin, for everyday fruit or Madeira cake is a must, a useful size is 20.5 cm/8 inches.

∾ **Metal Muffin Trays** – Muffin trays come in different weights and sizes; they are generally available with six or 12 deep-set holes. When purchasing, buy the heaviest type you can – although these will be expensive, they produce the best results, as they have good heat distribution and do not buckle. Muffin trays can vary in the size and depth of hole, which obviously affects the eventual size of the muffin.

If using trays without a nonstick finish, it is advisable to give these a light greasing before use. To grease trays, apply a thin film of melted vegetable margarine with a pastry brush or rub round the tin with kitchen paper and a little softened butter or margarine. You will normally need to line metal muffin trays with deep paper muffin cases or strips of baking parchment.

Silicone Muffin Trays and Cupcake Cases –
These are flexible and produce very good results. Although they are sold as nonstick, it is still advisable to rub round each hole or case with a little oil on kitchen paper to prevent sticking. Silicone cupcake cases come in many bright colours and, unlike paper cases, are reusable. Simply wash out any crumbs after use in soapy water and leave them to dry, or clean them in the dishwasher.

Paper Cases – These come in many varieties,
colours and shapes. It is advisable to buy the more expensive types, which are thicker and give a good shape to the cake as it rises. Oil and moisture is less likely to penetrate through the thicker cases, whereas it may show through the cheaper ones. Metallic gold, silver and coloured cupcake cases give good results and create a stunning effect for a special occasion. Cupcake cases also come in mini-muffin sizes. These may not be so easy to find but can be bought from mail-order cake decoration suppliers.

Baking Papers and Foil – Nonstick baking
'parchment' or 'paper' is useful for lining the bases of small tins or for drying out chocolate and sugarpaste shapes.

Greaseproof paper is needed for making triangular paper icing bags. Baking parchment can be used, but greaseproof paper is better, as it is thinner and more flexible.

A large sheet of kitchen foil is handy for wrapping cakes or for protecting wrapped cakes in the freezer.

Key Equipment

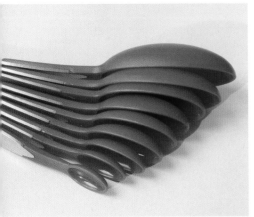

Useful Items

∾ **Mixing Bowls** – Three to four different sizes of mixing bowls are very useful for mixing and melting ingredients.

∾ **Wire Cooling Racks** – Another vital piece of equipment is a wire cooling rack. It is essential when baking to allow cakes to cool after being removed from their tins.

A wire rack also protects your kitchen surfaces from the heat and allows air to circulate around the goodies, speeding cooling and preventing soggy bottoms.

∾ **Measuring Items** – Baking needs 100 per cent accuracy to ensure a perfect result. Scales come in many shapes and sizes, both digital and with weights. Most have a weigh pan, although, with some, your own bowl is used. Measuring jugs and spoons are essential for accurate measuring of both your dry and wet ingredients.

∾ **Mixing Spoons and Sieves** – Basic mixing cutlery is also essential, such as a wooden spoon (for mixing and creaming), a spatula (for transferring the mixture from the mixing bowl to the baking tins and spreading the mixture once it is in the tins) and a palette knife (to ease cakes out of their tins before placing them on the wire racks to cool). Also, do not forget a fine-mesh sieve, for sifting flour and powders.

∾ Cake Tester or Skewer – Use a small thin metal skewer for inserting into the centre of a cake to test if the cake is ready. This is a handy piece of equipment but, if you do not have one, a clean thin metal knitting needle may be used instead.

∾ Pastry Brush – A pastry brush is used for brushing glazes over cakes and melted butter round tins. As brushes tend to wear out regularly and shed their bristles, keep a spare new brush to hand.

∾ Palette Knives – A small and a large palette knife are ideal for many jobs, including loosening cakes from their tins, lifting cakes and swirling on buttercream icing. A palette knife with a cranked blade is useful for lifting small cakes or flat pieces of sugarpaste.

∾ Kitchen Scissors – Scissors are essential for many small jobs, including cutting papers to size and snipping cherries, dried fruits or nuts into chunks.

∾ Grater – A grater is useful for grating citrus zests, chocolate and marzipan. Choose one with a fine and a coarse side.

∾ Stamps and Cutters – Stamps and cutters for almost any imaginable shape can be bought from specialist cake and baking stores. They come in classic metal cookie-cutter styles, in plastic, or as plunger-style. If you do not have appropriate cutters, there are some templates at the back of this book that can be used instead.

Key Equipment

∾ Piping Bags and Nozzles – A nylon piping bag that comes with a set of five nozzles is a very useful piece of equipment for decorating with icings. Look for a set with a plain nozzle and various star nozzles for piping swirls. The larger the star nozzle, the wider the swirls will be on the finished cake. Disposable paper or clear plastic icing bags are available, but nylon piping bags can be washed out in warm soapy water and dried out, ready to re-use again and again.

Electrical Equipment

Nowadays help from time-saving gadgets and electrical equipment makes baking far easier and quicker. There is a wide choice of machines available, from the most basic to the highly sophisticated.

∾ Food Processors – First decide what you need your processor to do when choosing a machine. If you are a novice, it may be a waste to start with a machine which offers a wide range of implements and functions. This can be off-putting and result in not using the machine to its ultimate potential. When buying a food processor, look for measurements on the sides of the processor bowl and machines with a removable feed tube, which allows food or liquid to be added while the motor is still running. Look out for machines that have the facility to increase the capacity of the bowl and have a pulse button for controlled chopping. For many, storage is an issue so reversible discs and flex storage, or, on more advanced models, a blade storage compartment or box, can be advantageous.

It is also worth thinking about machines which offer optional extras which can be bought as your cooking requirements change. Mini chopping bowls are available for those wanting to chop small quantities of food. If time is an issue, dishwasher-friendly attachments may be vital. Citrus presses, liquidisers and whisks may all be useful attachments for the individual cook.

∾ Table-top Mixers – Table-top mixers are freestanding and are capable of dealing with fairly large quantities of mixture. They are robust machines and good for heavy cake mixing as well as whipping cream, whisking egg whites or making one-stage cakes.

These mixers also offer a wide range of attachments ranging from liquidisers to mincers, juicers, can openers and many more and varied attachments.

∾ Hand-held Mixers – A hand-held electric mixer makes quick work of whisking butter and sugar and is an invaluable aid for cake baking. They are smaller than freestanding mixers and often come with their own bowl and stand from which they can be lifted off and used as hand-held devices. They have a motorised head with detachable twin whisks.

These mixers are versatile as they do not need a specific bowl in which to whisk. Any suitable mixing bowl can be used. Do not be tempted to use a food processor for mixing small amounts, as it is easy to over-process and this may produce flat cakes.

Basic Cake Making Techniques

Lining Cake Tins

If a recipe states that the tin needs lining, do not be tempted to ignore this. Rich fruit cakes and other cakes that take a long time to cook benefit from the tin being lined so that the edges and base do not burn or dry out. Greaseproof paper or baking parchment is ideal for this. It is a good idea to have the paper at least double thickness, or preferably 3–4 thicknesses. Sponge cakes and other cakes that are cooked in 30 minutes or less are also better if the bases are lined, as it is far easier to remove them from the tin.

The best way to line a round or square tin is to lightly draw around the base and then cut just inside the markings, making it easy to sit in the tin. Next, lightly grease the paper so that it will easily peel away from the cake.

If the sides of the tin also need to be lined, then cut a strip of paper long enough for the tin. This can be measured by wrapping a piece of string around the rim of the tin. Once again, lightly grease the paper, push against the tin and oil once more, as this will hold the paper to the sides of the tin.

Separating Eggs

When separating eggs (that is, separating the white from the yolk), crack an egg in half lightly and cleanly over a bowl, being careful not to break the yolk and keeping it in the shell. Then tip the yolk backwards and forwards between the two shell halves, allowing as much of the white as possible to spill out into the bowl. Keep or discard the yolk and/or the white as needed. Make sure that you do not get any yolk in your whites, as this will prevent successful whisking of the whites. It takes practice!

Different Making Methods

❧ Creaming – Light cakes are made by the creaming method, which means that the butter and sugar are first beaten or 'creamed' together. A little care is needed for this method. Using a large mixing bowl, beat the fat and sugar together until pale and fluffy. The eggs are gradually beaten in to form a slackened batter and the flour is folded in last, to stiffen up the mixture. In some recipes, egg whites are whisked and added to the mixture separately for extra lightness.

When the eggs are added, they are best used at room temperature to prevent the mixture from splitting or 'curdling'. Adding a teaspoon of flour with each beaten egg will help to keep the mixture light and smooth and prevent the mixture from separating. A badly mixed, curdled batter will hold less air and be heavy or can cause a sunken cake.

❧ All-in-one Mixtures – This 'one stage' method is quick and easy and is perfect for those new to baking, as it does not involve any complicated techniques.

It is ideal for making light sponges, but soft tub-type margarine or softened butter at room temperature must be used. There is no need for any creaming or rubbing in, as all the ingredients are simply placed in a large bowl and quickly beaten together for just a few minutes until smooth. Be careful not to over-beat, as this will make the mixture too wet. Self-raising flour with the addition of a little extra baking powder is vital for a good rise.

∾ Fruit Cakes – Rich fruit cakes are usually made by the creaming method, then dried fruits and nuts are folded in to the mixture last.

Checking to See if the Cakes Are Cooked

For light sponge-type cakes, press the centre lightly with the fingertips and, if the cake is cooked, it should spring back easily. To test more thoroughly, insert a thin warmed skewer into the deepest part of the centre.

If the cake is cooked it will come out perfectly cleanly with no mixture sticking to it but, if there is some on the skewer, bake the cakes for a little longer and test again.

Small cupcakes should be golden, risen and firm to the touch when pressed lightly in the centre. The last part of a cupcake to cook is the centre, so, after the baking time stated, check this area.

How to Patch Up Mistakes

If the cakes have overcooked or are burnt on the outside, simply scrape this away with a serrated knife and cover the surface with buttercream. If the cakes are a little dry, sprinkle them with a few drops of sweet sherry or orange juice.

Cutting the Tops Level

Many cakes and cupcakes form a small peak while baking. However, some methods of decorating cakes require a flat surface, so, for these, trim the tops level with a knife. You can also coat cupcakes with apricot glaze and press on a disc of almond paste or sugarpaste to give a flat surface to decorate.

Storing Cakes

Chocolate and Madeira cakes can be made ahead of time and will store well for up to five days before decorating. Cover in fresh baking parchment then wrap in foil and keep in a cool place, or alternately, freeze for up to two months.

Rich fruit cakes should be stored before cutting and need at least one month for the flavour to mature. Wedding cakes should be made three months ahead to give them a better flavour and enable the cake to be moist enough to cut cleanly into slices. Wrap rich fruit cakes in their baking papers, then overwrap in clean baking parchment then a double layer of foil and seal with tape. Keep the cakes in a cool place until required.

Basic Cake Recipes

Rich Fruit Cake

Square Cake Size	13 cm/5 inch square	16 cm/6 inch square	18 cm/7 inch square
Round Cake Size	15 cm/6 inch round	18 cm/7 inch round	20 cm/8 inch round
sultanas	125 g/4 oz	175 g/6 oz	225 g/8 oz
raisins	125 g/4 oz	175 g/6 oz	225 g/8 oz
currants	125 g/4 oz	175 g/6 oz	225 g/8 oz
chopped mixed peel	50 g/2 oz	75 g/3 oz	125 g/4oz
glace cherries, chopped	50 g/2 oz	75 g/3 oz	125 g/4 oz
lemons	$1/2$	$1/2$	1
dark rum or fresh orange juice	2 tbsp	3 tbsp	4 tbsp
butter, softened	125 g/4oz	175 g/6 oz	225 g/8 oz
soft dark muscovado sugar	125 g/4oz	175 g/6 oz	225 g/8 oz
plain flour	125 g/4oz	175 g/6 oz	225 g/ 8 oz
mixed spice	$1/2$ tsp	1 tsp	2 tsp
ground almonds	25 g/ 1oz	50 g/ 2oz	75 g/3 oz
eggs, beaten	2	3	4–5
dark treacle	2 tsp	1 tbsp	1 tbsp
Cooking time 1	30 mins	50 mins	1 hour
Cooking time 2	1 hour 30 mins	1 hour 40 mins	$2^1/4$ hours

Square Cake Size	20 cm/8 inch square	23cm/9 inch square	25 cm/10 inch square
Round Cake Size	23 cm/9 inch round	25 cm/10 inch round	28 cm/11 inch round
sultanas	275 g/10 oz	350 g/12oz	450 g/1 b
raisins	275 g/10oz	350 g/12 oz	450 g/1lb
currants	275 g/10 oz	350 g/12 oz	450 g/1 lb
chopped mixed peel	150 g/5 oz	175 g/5 oz	200 g/7oz
glace cherries, chopped	150 g/5 oz	175 g/6 oz	200 g/7oz
lemons	1	$1^1/_2$	2
dark rum or fresh orange juice	2 tbsp	4 tbsp	6 tbsp
butter, softened	275 g/10 oz	350 g/12 oz	450 g/1 lb
soft dark muscovado sugar	275 g/10 oz	350 g/12 oz	450 g/1 lb
plain flour	275 g/10oz	350 g/12 oz	450 g/ 1 lb
mixed spice	15 ml/1 tbsp	15 ml/1 tbsp	15 ml/ 1 tbsp
ground almonds	125 g/4 oz	125 g/ 4oz	150 g/5 oz
eggs, beaten	5–6	6	8
dark treacle	1 tbsp	1 tbsp	2 tbsp
Cooking time 1	1 hour 30 mins	1 hour 50 mins	2 hours
Cooking time 2	$2^1/_2$–3 hours	3 hours	$3^1/_4$ hours

Basic Cake Recipes

Before you start to bake, place the sultanas, raisins, currants, peel and cherries in a large bowl. Finely grate in the zest from the lemon and add the dark rum or freshly squeezed orange juice. Stir, cover and leave to soak overnight or for 24 hours if possible.

Preheat the oven to 150°C/300°F/Gas Mark 2. Grease and line the tin with a treble layer of nonstick baking parchment.

Cream the butter and muscovado sugar in a large bowl until light and fluffy. Sift the flour and mixed spice together in a separate bowl, then stir in the ground almonds.

Add the eggs to the creamed mixture, a little at a time, adding a teaspoon of flour with each addition. Fold the remaining flour into the bowl then add the treacle and soaked fruits. Stir well until the mixture is soft, smooth and well blended.

Spoon the mixture into the tin, then make a hollow in the centre of the mixture with the back of large spoon.

Tie a layer of newspaper round the outside of the tin and bake according to cooking time 1, then reduce the heat to 120°C/250°F/Gas Mark 1/2 for cooking time 2.

If the top of the large cake starts to overbrown, cover with a layer of damp crumpled baking parchment. Test the cake by inserting a skewer into the centre, which should come out with no mixture sticking to it.

Cool the cake in the tin and then remove, leaving the lining papers on. Wrap the cake in an extra layer of baking parchment, then tightly in foil and leave to mature for 1–3 months in a cool place.

Rich Chocolate Cake

Square Cake Size	13 cm/5 inch square	18 cm/7 inch square	23 cm/9 inch square
Round Cake Size	15 cm/6 inch round	20 cm/8 inch round	25 cm/10 inch round
Plain Chocolate	50 g/2 oz	125 g/4 oz	225 g/8 oz
Soft Dark Brown Sugar	150 g/5 oz	275 g/10 oz	550 g/1^1/$_4$ lb
Milk	110 ml/4^1/$_2$ fl oz	200 ml/7 fl oz	500 ml/17 fl oz
Butter, softened	50 g/2oz	125 g/4 oz	225 g/8 oz
Eggs, beaten	1	3	6
Plain Flour	125 g/4oz	225 g/8 oz	450 g/1 lb
Bicarbonate of Soda	^{1}/$_2$ tsp	1 tsp	2 tsp
Cooking time	45 mins	1 hour	1^1/$_2$ hours

Preheat the oven to 180°C/350°F/Gas Mark 4. Grease and line the tin with nonstick baking parchment. Break the chocolate into small pieces and place in a heavy-based pan with one third of the sugar and all of the milk. Heat gently until the chocolate has melted then remove from the heat and cool.

Beat the butter and remaining sugar together until fluffy then beat in the eggs a little at a time. Gradually beat in the cold melted chocolate mixture.

Sift the flour and bicarbonate of soda into the mixture and fold together with a large metal spoon until smooth. Bake for the time shown on the chart or until a skewer inserted in the centre comes out cleanly.

Cool for 10 minutes then turn out of the tin onto a wire rack to cool. Store wrapped in foil until needed or freeze wrapped tightly in foil for up to three months.

Madeira Cake

Square Cake Size	13 cm/5 inch square	16 cm/6 inch square	18 cm/7 inch square
Round Cake Size	15 cm/6 inch round	18 cm/7 inch round	20 cm/8 inch round
butter, softened	175 g/6 oz	225 g/8 oz	350 g/12 oz
caster sugar	175 g/6 oz	225 g/8 oz	350 g/12 oz
self-raising flour	175 g/6 oz	225 g/8 oz	350 g/12 oz
plain flour	75 g/3oz	125 g/4 oz	175 g/ 6 oz
eggs	3	4	6
vanilla extract	$1/2$ tsp	1 tsp	1 tsp
glycerine	1 tsp	1 tsp	1 tsp
Cooking time	1 hour	1–$1^1/4$ hours	$1^1/4$–$1^1/2$ hours

Square Cake Size	20 cm/8 inch square	23 cm/9 inch square
Round Cake Size	23 cm/9 inch round	25 cm/10 inch round
butter, softened	450 g/1 lb	500 g/1 lb 2 oz
caster sugar	450 g/1 lb	500 g/1 lb 2 oz
self-raising flour	450 g/1 lb	500 g/1 lb 2 oz
plain flour	225 g/8oz	250 g/9 oz
eggs	8	9
vanilla extract	2 tsp	1 tbsp
glycerine	2 tsp	1 tbsp
Cooking time	$1^1/2$ – $1^3/4$ hours	$1^1/2$ – $1^3/4$ hours

Preheat the oven to 160°C/325°F/Gas Mark 3. Grease and line the tin with nonstick baking parchment.

Cream the butter and caster sugar in a large bowl until light and fluffy. Sift the flours together. Whisk the eggs into the mixture one at a time, adding a teaspoon of flour with each to prevent the mixture from curdling.

Add the remaining flour, vanilla extract and glycerine to the mixture and fold together with a large metal spoon until the mixture is smooth.

Spoon into the tin and bake for the time shown on the chart until firm and well risen and a skewer inserted into the centre comes out cleanly.

Leave to cool in the tin for 10 minutes then turn out onto a wire rack to cool. Wrap in foil and store for up to three days before decorating. Freeze, wrapped in foil for up to two months.

- Bowl Shaped – To cook the cake in a 2 litre/4 pint ovenproof bowl, grease the bowl well and use the amounts for the 13 cm/5 inch square cake, baking for 45 minutes–1 hour.

- Lemon Variation – To make the lemon variation of the Madeira cake, you can simply omit the vanilla extract and add the same amount of finely grated lemon zest.

- Almond Variation – To make the almond variation of the Madeira cake, you can simply omit the vanilla extract and add the same amount of almond extract.

Basic Cake Recipes

Basic Vanilla Cupcakes

Makes 12–14

125 g/4 oz caster sugar
125 g/4 oz soft tub margarine
2 medium eggs
125 g/4 oz self-raising flour
½ tsp baking powder
½ tsp vanilla extract

Preheat the oven to 190˚C/350˚F/Gas Mark 5. Line a
bun tray with paper cases.

Place all the cupcake ingredients in a large bowl and
beat with an electric mixer for about 2 minutes until light
and smooth. Fill the paper cases halfway up with the
mixture. Bake for about 15 minutes until firm, risen
and golden.

Remove to a wire rack to cool. Keeps for 2–3 days in a
lidded container. Can be frozen for up to two months but the paper cases will come away when
thawed and these will need replacing.

❧ Chocolate Variation – Omit the caster sugar and use soft light brown sugar instead. Sift
25 g/1oz cocoa powder in with the flour, and baking powder. Omit the vanilla extract and add 2
tbsp milk instead. Mix and bake as above.

❧ Cherry & Almond Variation – Add 50 g/2 oz finely chopped washed glacé cherries.
Omit the vanilla extract and use almond extract instead. Mix and bake as above.

Decorating
Basics

No cake would be complete without a touch of icing, the more the better we say! This is where you can let your imagination run riot and create literally whatever you fancy! With basic decorating ingredients and techniques, as well as key icing recipes, such as the classic Cream Cheese Frosting and that all important Sugarpaste Icing, it won't be long before you'll be a master of cake decorating.

Decorating Ingredients

There are a multitude of ingredients you can use to decorate your cakes. Below you will find reference to many of the icings, colourings and edible decorations you can buy, as well as key icing recipes which will show you how to whip up your own icings from scratch. These basic icing recipes will be referenced often throughout the main cake decorating chapters.

∾ **Icing Sugar** – Icing sugar is fine and powdery. It is usually sold plain and white, but can also be bought as an unrefined golden (or 'natural') variety. Use it for delicate icings, frostings and decorations. Store this sugar in a dry place, as it can absorb moisture and this will make it go hard and lumpy. Always sift this sugar at least once, or preferably twice, before you use it, to remove any hard lumps that would prevent icing from achieving a smooth texture – lumpy icing is impossible to pipe out.

∾ **Fondant Icing Sugar** – This is sold in plain and flavoured varieties and gives a beautiful glossy finish to cake toppings. Just add a little boiled water to the sugar, according to the packet instructions, to make a shiny icing that can be poured or drizzled over cake tops to give a very professional finish. Colour the plain white icing with a few spots of paste food colour to achieve your desired result.

Flavoured fondant icing sugar is sold in strawberry, raspberry, orange, lemon and blackcurrant flavours and also has colouring added. These sugars are ideal if you want to make a large batch of cakes with different coloured and flavoured toppings. Flavoured fondant sugars can also be whisked with softened unsalted butter and cream cheese to make delicious frostings in just a few moments.

∾ Royal Icing Sugar – Royal icing sets to a classic, firm Christmas-cake-style covering. Sold in packs as plain white sugar, this is whisked with cold water to give an instant royal icing. It has dried egg white included in the mixture, so does not need the long beating that traditional royal icing recipes require. It is also ideal to use for those who cannot eat raw egg whites.

∾ Tubes of Writing Icing – You can buy small tubes of ready-coloured royal icing or gel icing, usually in sets of black, red, yellow and blue, and these are ideal for small amounts of writing or for piping on dots or small decorations.

∾ Food Colourings – You can buy food colourings in liquid, paste, gel and powder or dust forms in a great range of colours.

Paste food colours are best for using with sugarpaste. These are sold in small tubs and are very concentrated, so should be added to the sugarpaste dot by dot on the end of a wooden cocktail stick. Knead the colouring in evenly, adding more until you get the colour you require.

Liquid and gel food colourings are ideal for adding to frostings. Add this cautiously drop by drop, beating the frosting well until you reach the colour you require.

Dusts and sparkle colourings should be lightly brushed onto dry sugarpaste to form a delicate sheen to decorations such as flowers.

∾ Bought Sugar Decorations and Sprinkles – A range of sprinkles can be bought in supermarkets or by mail order from specialist cake decorating companies, and these provide a wonderful way to make quick and easy cake toppings.

Basic Buttercream Frosting

Covers a 20 cm/8 inch round cake or 12 small cakes

Ingredients

150 g/5 oz unsalted butter, softened at room temperature
225 g/8 oz icing sugar, sifted
2 tbsp hot milk or water
1 tsp vanilla extract
food colourings of choice

Beat the butter until light and fluffy, then beat in the sifted icing sugar and hot milk or water in two batches.

Add the vanilla extract and any colourings. Store, chilled for up to two days in a lidded container.

Variations
Omit the vanilla extract and instead:

- **Coffee** – Blend 2 tsp coffee extract with the milk.

- **Chocolate** – Blend 2 tbsp cocoa powder to a paste with 2 tbsp boiling water and use instead of the hot milk or water.

Sugarpaste Icing

Makes 350 g/12 oz to cover a 20 cm/8 inch round cake or 12 small cakes or use for decorations

Ingredients

1 medium egg white
1 tbsp liquid glucose
350 g/12 oz icing sugar, sifted, plus extra for dusting

Place the egg white and liquid glucose in a large mixing bowl and stir together, breaking up the egg white.

Add the icing sugar gradually, mixing in until the mixture binds together and forms a ball.

Turn the ball of icing out onto a clean surface dusted with icing sugar and knead for 5 minutes until soft but firm enough to roll out.

If the icing is too soft, knead in a little more icing sugar until the mixture is pliable.

To colour, knead in paste food colouring. Do not use liquid food colour, as this is not suitable and will make the sugarpaste limp.

To use, roll out thinly on a clean surface dusted with icing sugar to a circle large enough to cover a cake or cut out discs large enough to cover the top of each cupcake.

Flower Paste

Ingredients

2 tsp powdered gelatine
2 tsp liquid glucose
2 tsp white vegetable fat
450g/1 lb sifted icing sugar
1 tsp gum tragacanth powder
1 egg white

Flower or petal paste is used for making really thin, delicate flowers and decorations and these will set hard so that they can be handled easily.

Flower paste will roll out much more thinly than sugarpaste and is worth using for wedding cakes as it gives a realistic finish to flowers and these can be made ahead of time and easily stored. It can be bought from cake decorating suppliers or by mail order in small ready made slabs in different colours or as a powder that can be reconstituted with a little cold water and made into a paste.

To make your own, follow the recipe and store the paste in the refrigerator tightly wrapped in strong plastic until needed.

Place 1^1/$_2$ tsp cold water in a heatproof bowl. Sprinkle over the gelatine and add the liquid glucose and white fat. Place the bowl over a saucepan of hot water and heat until melted, stirring occasionally. Cool slightly.

Sift the icing sugar and gum tragacanth powder into a bowl, make a well in the centre and add the egg white and the cooled gelatine mixture. Mix together to make a soft paste.

Knead the paste on a surface dusted with icing sugar until smooth then wrap in clingfilm to exclude all air. Leave for 2 hours then break off small pieces and use to make fine flowers and petals.

Cream Cheese Frosting

Covers a 20 cm/8 inch round cake or 12 small cakes

Ingredients

50 g/2 oz unsalted butter, softened at room temperature
300 g/11 oz icing sugar, sifted
flavouring of choice
food colourings of choice
125 g/4 oz full-fat cream cheese

Beat the butter and icing sugar together until light and fluffy.

Add flavourings and colourings of choice and beat again.

Add the cream cheese and whisk until light and fluffy.

Do not over-beat, however, as the mixture can become runny.

Royal Icing

Makes 500 g/1 lb 2 oz to cover a 20 cm/8 inch round cake or 12 small cakes

Ingredients

2 medium egg whites
500 g/1 lb 2 oz icing sugar, sifted
2 tsp lemon juice

Put the egg whites in a large bowl and whisk lightly with a fork to break up the whites until foamy.

Sift in half the icing sugar with the lemon juice and beat well with an electric mixer for 4 minutes or by hand with a wooden spoon for about 10 minutes until smooth.

Gradually sift in the remaining icing sugar and beat again until thick, smooth and brilliant white and the icing forms soft peaks when flicked up with a spoon.

Keep the royal icing covered with a clean damp cloth until ready for use, or store in the refrigerator in a lidded plastic container until needed.

If making royal icing to use later, beat it again before use to remove any air bubbles that may have formed in the mixture.

Modelling Chocolate

Ingredients

125 g/4 oz plain, milk or
white chocolate
2 tbsp liquid glucose

Break the chocolate into small pieces and melt in a
heatproof bowl standing over a pan of warm water.

Remove from the heat and beat in the liquid glucose until a
paste forms that comes away from the sides of the bowl.

Place the paste in a plastic bag and chill for 1 hour until
firm, or store for up to two weeks in a tightly sealed
plastic bag.

To use, break off pieces and knead until pliable. Modelling
chocolate is ideal for making thin ribbons and flowers.

Chocolate Covering Icing

To cover a 20 cm/8 inch round cake

Ingredients

175 g/6 oz dark chocolate
2 tbsp liquid glucose
1 medium egg white
500 g/1 lb 2 oz sifted icing sugar

Break up the chocolate into pieces and melt in a heatproof bowl standing over a bowl of warm water. Add the liquid glucose and stir until melted.

Remove from the heat and cool for 5 minutes then whisk in the egg white and half the sugar until smooth. When the mixture becomes stiff, turn out onto a flat surface and knead in the remaining icing sugar.

Wrap tightly in clingfilm and keep in a cool place for up to three days. To use, break off pieces and knead until soft and warm. Use quickly, as when the paste cools it will start to harden more quickly than sugarpaste.

Apricot Glaze Almond Paste

**Makes 450 g/1 lb to cover
2 x 20 cm/8 inch round
cakes, or 24 small cakes**

For the Apricot Glaze:

450 g/1 lb apricot jam
3 tbsp water
1 tsp lemon juice

For the Almond Paste:

125 g/4 oz sifted icing sugar
125 g/4 oz caster sugar
225 g/8 oz ground almonds
1 medium egg
1 tsp lemon juice

For the Apricot Glaze, place the jam, water and juice in a heavy-based saucepan and heat gently, stirring, until soft and melted.

Boil rapidly for 1 minute, then press through a fine sieve with the back of a wooden spoon. Discard the pieces of fruit.

Use immediately for glazing or sticking on almond paste, or pour into a clean jar or plastic lidded container and store in the refrigerator for up to three months.

For the Almond Paste, stir the sugars and ground almonds together in a bowl. Whisk the egg and lemon juice together and mix into the dry ingredients.

Knead until the paste is smooth. Wrap tightly in clingfilm or foil to keep airtight and store in the refrigerator until needed. The paste can be made 2–3 days ahead of time but, after that, it will start to dry out and become difficult to handle.

To use the paste, knead on a surface dusted with icing sugar. Brush the top of each cake with apricot glaze. Roll out the almond paste to a circle large enough to cover the cake or cut out discs large enough to cover the tops of the cupcakes. Press onto the cakes.

Glacé Icing

**Covers a 20 cm/8 inch
round cake (top)
or 12 small cakes**

Ingredients

225 g/8 oz icing sugar
few drops of lemon juice, vanilla
or almond extract
2–3 tbsp boiling water

Sift the icing sugar into a bowl and add the chosen flavouring then gradually stir in enough water to mix to a consistency of thick cream.

Beat with a wooden spoon until the icing is thick enough to coat the back of the spoon. Use immediately as the icing will begin to from a skin as it stars to set.

Decorating Techniques

Covering Cakes

∾ **With Almond Paste** – Remove all the papers in which the cake was baked, and if necessary, trim the top of the cake level if it has peaked. Brush the top and sides of the cake with apricot glaze.

Sprinkle a clean flat surface with icing sugar and knead one third of the almond paste. Measure the circumference of the cake or the length of one side with a piece of string. Using the string as a guide, roll the paste into a strip long enough to go round the cake and wide enough to cover the sides.

Roll the paste up into a coil and press one end onto the side of the cake. Unroll the paste, pressing into the sides of the cake as you go round.

Knead the remaining paste and roll out to the same shape as the top of the cake, plus an overlap of 1 cm/½ inch. Lay the paste on top of the cake and press down, moulding the overlap on the sides together to give a good edge to the top. Flatten the top and sides with a small rolling pin or an icing smoother and leave to dry out for 24 hours before icing.

∾ **With Sugarpaste Icing** – If covered in almond paste, brush the paste lightly with a little boiled water. If using buttercream or apricot glaze, spread these over the trimmed cake to give a surface for the sugarpaste to stick to.

Knead the sugarpaste until softened, then roll into a ball. Roll out the sugarpaste to about 1 cm/^{1}/$_2$ inch thickness on a flat surface lightly dusted with icing sugar, moving the sugarpaste occasionally to prevent it from sticking to the surface.

Measure the circumference of the cake with string and roll the sugar paste 2.5 cm/2 inch larger in order to cover the whole cake. Lift the sugarpaste carefully onto the cake holding it flat with your palms until it is central.

Dust your hands with icing sugar and smooth the icing down over the top and sides of the cake fluting out the bottom edges. Do not pleat the icing as this will leave a line. Smooth down to remove any air bubbles under the surface of the icing, then trim the edges with a sharp knife.

Using the flat of your hand or an icing smoother, flatten out the top and sides using a circular movement. Do not wear any rings, as these will leave ridges in the soft icing. Gather up the trimmings into a ball and keep these tightly wrapped in a plastic bag.

With Royal Icing – Make sure the almond paste has dried out for 24 hours, or oil from the paste may seep into the icing.

Place a large spoonful of icing in the centre of the cake and smooth out using a palette knife in a paddling movement to get rid of any air bubbles.

Draw an icing rule across the top of the cake towards you at an angle. Repeat, pulling back and forth, until the icing is flat. Remove any surplus icing round the top edges and leave to dry out for 24 hours. Keep the remaining icing covered in a plastic box with a tightly fitted lid. To cover the sides, for best results, place the cake on an icing

Decorating Techniques

turntable. Spread a layer of icing round the sides, using the same paddling motion as the top. Smooth the surface roughly then, holding an icing scraper at a 45 degree angle, rotate the cake, keeping the scraper still. Rotate the cake until the sides are flat, then carefully lift away any excess icing with a palette knife to give a clean top edge. Leave to dry out for 24 hours. Repeat, adding another layer of royal icing to give a smooth surface for decorating.

Dowelling Tiered Cakes

For large tiered cakes you will need to insert small sticks of wooden or plastic dowelling into the lower tiers to take the weight of the next layer and stop this sinking.

First decide where you want to position the dowels. Cover the cake with almond paste and sugarpaste and place centrally on a board. Place a sheet of baking parchment over the cake, cut to the size of the top of the cake. Decide where you want the dowels to go and mark 4 equal dots in a square, centrally on the paper.

Replace the paper and mark through each dot with a skewer. Remove the paper and push a piece of dowel down into the cake at each mark. Make a mark with a pencil where the dowel comes out of the cake. Pull the dowels out of the cake and using a serrated knife, trim them to 1 mm/¹⁄₃₂ inch above the pencil mark. Replace the dowels in the cake and ensure these are all to 1 mm. If not, trim them again, then place the next tier of the cake on top. Repeat if using three tiers.

Crystallising Petals, Flowers, Leaves and Berries

Wash and dry herbs and leaves such as rosemary sprigs and small bay leaves or berries such as cranberries. Separate edible petals from small flowers such as rosebuds and clean small flowers such as violets with a clean brush, but do not wash them. Beat 1 medium egg white with 2 tsp cold water until frothy. Paint a thin layer of egg white carefully over the items (*see* picture top right), then sprinkle lightly with caster sugar (*see* picture bottom right), shaking to remove any excess. Leave to dry on a wire rack lined with nonstick baking parchment.

Using Buttercream and Cream Cheese Frostings

These soft icings can be swirled onto the tops of cakes with a small palette knife or placed in a piping bag fitted with a star nozzle to pipe impressive whirls, such as when you want to finish off your cake with a piped border or simply add those elegant flourishes.

∽ Do not be mean with the amount of frosting you use. If this is scraped on thinly, you will see the cake underneath, so be generous.

∽ Keep cakes with frostings in a cool place, or refrigerate, as they contain a high percentage of butter, which will melt easily in too warm a place.

∽ Cakes coated in buttercream can be decorated easily with colourful sprinkles and sugars. This is easy with cupcakes. Place the sprinkles in a small saucer or on a piece of nonstick baking parchment and roll the outside edges of each cupcake in the decorations.

Decorating Techniques

Make a Paper Icing Bag

Cut out a 38 x 25.5 cm/15 x 10 inch rectangle of greaseproof paper. Fold it diagonally in half to form 2 triangular shapes. Cut along the fold line to make 2 triangles. One of these triangles can be used another time – it is quicker and easier to make two at a time from one square than to measure and mark out a triangle on a sheet of paper.

Fold one of the points on the long side of the triangle over the top to make a sharp cone and hold in the centre. Fold the other sharp end of the triangle over the cone. Hold all the points together at the back of the cone, keeping the pointed end sharp. Turn the points inside the top edge, fold over to make a crease, then secure with a piece of sticky tape.

To use, snip away the end, place a piping nozzle in position and fill the bag with icing, or fill the bag with icing first, then snip away a tiny hole at the end for piping a plain edge, writing or piping tiny dots.

Piping Flowers with Royal Icing

Cut small squares of waxed paper and attach each one to an icing nail with a dot of royal icing.

To pipe a rose, half fill a small piping bag fitted with a flower nozzle and holding the nozzle with the thinnest part uppermost, pipe a small cone onto the paper to form the rosebud. Pipe petals round the rosebud onto the paper, overlapping each one and curling the edge away. Leave the roses to dry out for 12 hours, then peel away from the paper to use, or store in an airtight container between layers of parchment until needed.

To pipe a daisy, work with the thick edge of the nozzle towards the centre and pipe 5 even sized petals so that they meet in a star shape. Pipe a round dot in the centre in a contrasting colour and leave to dry out as above.

Using Sugarpaste

Sugarpaste is a versatile icing, as it can be used for covering whole cakes or modelling all sorts of fancy decorations. To use as a covering, roll out the sugarpaste thinly on a surface dusted with icing sugar and use to cover the cake or cut out circles the size of the cupcake tops. Coat each cake with a little apricot glaze or buttercream and press on the circles to form a flat surface.

∾ To Copy Patterns from the Templates – At the back of this book, you will find templates for some of the shapes used in this book. Trace the pattern you want onto a sheet of clear greaseproof paper or nonstick baking parchment. Roll out the sugarpaste thinly, then position the traced pattern. Mark over the pattern with the tip of a small sharp knife or a pin. Remove the paper and cut out the marked-on pattern with a small sharp knife.

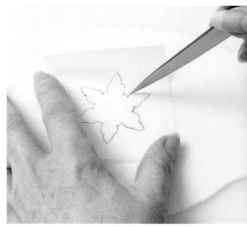

Decorating Techniques

Making Bows – Roll out the sugarpaste thinly on a surface lightly dusted with icing sugar, and with a knife cut out long thin narrow strips (*see* picture top left).

Roll small squares of baking parchment into narrow tubes, or line the handle of a wooden spoon with clingfilm. Fold the icing over the paper or handle to form loops (*see* picture centre left) and leave to dry and harden for 2 hours, then carefully remove the paper or spoon handle.

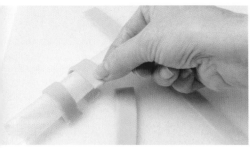

To make bows that are placed directly onto the cake, fill the centre of each loop with cotton wool balls, then remove these when the icing is firm.

Making Flat Decorations – To make letters, numbers or flat decorations, roll out the sugarpaste thinly and cut out the shapes. Leave to dry on nonstick baking parchment on a flat surface or a tray for 2–3 hours to make them firm and easy to handle.

Making Roses – Colour the sugarpaste icing with pink paste food colouring. Take a small piece of sugarpaste and make a small cone shape, then roll a small pea-sized piece of sugarpaste into a ball. Flatten out the ball into a petal shape and wrap this round the cone shape.

Continue adding more petals (*see* picture bottom left), then trim the thick base. Leave to dry for 2 hours in a clean egg box lined with foil or clingfilm.

Making Lilies – Lilies of all sizes can make elegant decorations for cakes (*see* Elegant Lilies Cake, page 136 for example).

Colour a little sugarpaste a deep yellow and mould this into thin sausage shapes. Leave these to firm on nonstick baking parchment or clingfilm for 2 hours.

Thinly roll out white sugarpaste and mark out small squares of 4 x 4 cm/1$^1\!/_2$ x 1$^1\!/_2$ inches. Wrap each square round a yellow centre to form a lily *(see* picture top right) and press the end together. Place the lilies on nonstick baking parchment to dry out for 2 hours.

Making Daisies – Daisies of all sizes are a popular flower to be found on decorated cakes (*see* Daisies Cupcakes, page 86 for example).

To model from sugarpaste, roll out a little sugarpaste thinly and, using a daisy stamp cutter, press out small flower shapes and mould these into a curve.

Leave the daisies to dry out on nonstick baking parchment, then pipe dots into the centre of each one with yellow royal icing or a small gel tube of writing icing (*see* picture centre right).

Making Butterfly Wings – Colour the sugarpaste and roll out thinly. Trace round the butterfly patterns and cut out the wing shapes (*see* picture bottom right). Leave these to dry, flat, on nonstick baking parchment for 4 hours to make them firm and easy to lift.

Decorating Techniques

Making Ruffles – To make frills and ruffles, roll out the sugarpaste on a surface lightly dusted with icing sugar and stamp out a fluted circle 6 cm/2½ inches wide with a pastry cutter. Cut away a small plain disc 3 cm/1 inch wide from the centre, and discard (*see* picture top left). Take a cocktail stick and roll this back and forth until the sugarpaste begins to frill up (*see* picture centre left).

Decorating Tips

∞ Always roll out almond paste or sugarpaste on a surface lightly dusted with icing sugar.

∞ Leave sugarpaste-covered cakes to firm up for 2 hours before adding decorations, as this provides a good finished surface to work on.

∞ Tie ribbons round the finished cake and secure them with a dab of royal icing. Never use pins in ribbons on a cake.

∞ Once decorated, store sugarpaste-covered cakes in large boxes in a cool place. Do not store in a refrigerator, as the sugarpaste will become damp and colours may run.

∞ Paste food colourings are best for working with sugarpaste and a little goes a very long way. As these are very concentrated, use a cocktail stick to add dots of paste gradually, until you are sure of the colour, and knead in until even.

Working With Chocolate

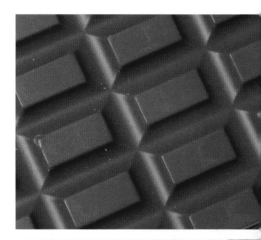

∾ **Melting Chocolate** – Care and attention is needed to melt chocolate for baking and cake decorating needs. If the chocolate gets too hot or comes into contact with water or steam, it will 'seize' or stiffen and form into a hard ball instead of a smooth melted mixture. You can add a little vegetable oil or margarine, a teaspoon at a time, to the mixture to make it liquid again.

To melt chocolate, break the bar into small pieces, or grate or chop it, and place in a heatproof bowl standing over a bowl of warm, not hot, water. Make sure the bowl containing the chocolate is completely dry and that steam or water cannot enter the bowl. Heat the water to a gentle simmer only and leave the bowl to stand for about 5 minutes. Do not let the water get too hot or the chocolate will reach too high a temperature and will lose its sheen.

The microwave oven is ideal for melting chocolate. Place the chocolate pieces in a small microwave-proof bowl and melt gently on low or defrost settings in small bursts of 30 seconds, checking and stirring in between, until the chocolate has melted.

∾ **Shaved Chocolate** – Chocolate shavings can add something special to finish off a cake. Using a vegetable peeler, shave a thick block of chocolate to make mini-curls. These are best achieved if the chocolate is a little soft, otherwise it has a tendency to break into little flakes.

∾ Decorating Techniques

Simple  Elegant Cakes

Some of the best cakes are those which are simple in construction, elegant in design and not to mention scrumptious to taste! Why not begin with a Soft Lacework Cake, simple in design yet beautiful to behold; or how about a Gameboard Cake, a fun accessory to any night in! To add elements of sophistication, give the Rose Petal Cake a try – it is guaranteed to impress even the fiercest of critics!

Rose Lily Bouquet Cake

Serves 12–14

For the cake base:

1 x 20 cm/8 inch round Madeira
cake (*see* page 30)
3 tbsp apricot glaze

To decorate:

900 g/2 lb ready-to-roll
sugarpaste icing
icing sugar, for dusting
yellow, pink and green paste
food colouring
2 tbsp royal icing

Trim the top of the cake flat if it has peaked and brush the glaze over the top and sides of the cake. Knead 550 g/1¼ lb of white sugarpaste into a round ball and flatten out. Roll out on a surface lightly dusted with icing sugar to a circle large enough to cover the top and sides of the cake. Using both hands, carefully lift over the cake and smooth down over the top and sides. Trim round the edges then place the cake on a 25 cm/10 in cake board or flat serving plate.

Colour 15 g/½ oz sugarpaste yellow, 175 g/6 oz pink and 50 g/2 oz green. Mould the yellow sugarpaste into long thin sausages and leave to firm on nonstick baking parchment for 2 hours. Roll out the white sugarpaste thinly, cut out 3 squares and wrap each square round a yellow centre to form a lily *(see* page 63). Leave to dry out on nonstick baking parchment for 2 hours.

Mould the remaining pink sugarpaste into 3 large roses (*see* page 64) and leave for 2–3 hours in egg boxes lined with crumped foil until firm. Roll small scraps of pink sugarpaste into 4 rosebuds and leave to harden for 2–3 hours. Using the green sugarpaste, cut out 10 leaves and mark veins on them using a sharp knife. When dry attach the flowers to one side of the cake with dabs of royal icing. Trim the base of the cake with a silk ribbon.

Pink Daisy Cake

Serves 12–14

For the cake base:

1 x 20 cm/8 inch round rich fruit cake (*see* page 26), covered in almond paste (*see* page 56)

To decorate:

2 batches royal icing (*see* page 46)
pink paste food colouring
125 g/4 oz ready-to-roll sugarpaste icing
icing sugar, for dusting

Place the cake on a 25 cm/10 inch plate or cake board. Colour three quarters of the royal icing pale pink and spread half on top of the cake and work it over the surface with a paddling movement. Draw an icing ruler across the top of the cake at an angle and smooth back and forth until completely flat then leave the top to dry out for 4 hours.

Store the remaining royal icing in a plastic box with a tight-fitting lid or cover the bowl with a clean damp cloth. Ice the sides with the remaining pink icing. Remove any surplus icing and leave to dry out for 24 hours.

Roll out the sugarpaste thinly on a surface lightly dusted with icing sugar and stamp out 12 large daisies with a daisy cutter. Place the daisies on a sheet of nonstick baking parchment and pipe a small pink dot in the centre of each one. Leave to dry out for 24 hours.

Place the remaining white royal icing in a piping bag fitted with a medium plain nozzle. Pipe a border of small dots round the base of the cake then pipe dots over the top and sides. Dab the underside of each daisy with a little royal icing and stick round the top edge of the cake to form a border.

Quilted Cupcakes

Makes 12

For the cakes:

1 batch vanilla cupcakes
(*see* page 32)

To decorate:

1 batch buttercream
(*see* page 38)
450 g/1 lb ready-to-roll sugarpaste
icing sugar, for dusting
edible gold or silver balls

Trim the tops of the cupcakes flat if they have peaked slightly.

Lightly coat the top of each cupcake with a little buttercream.

Roll out the sugarpaste on a surface lightly dusted with icing sugar and stamp out circles 6 cm/2½ inches wide (*see* page 251). Place these on the buttercream to cover the top of each cupcake.

Take a palette knife and press lines into the icing, then mark across in the opposite direction to make small squares. Place an edible gold or silver ball into the corner of each square.

Gameboard Cake

Serves 12

For the cake base:

1 x 20 cm/8 inch square Madeira cake (*see* page 30)

To decorate:

2 batches buttercream (*see* page 38)
550 g/1 lb 4 oz ready-to-roll sugarpaste icing
lilac and pink paste food colouring
icing sugar, for dusting

Trim the top of the cake flat if it has peaked. Cut the cake in half horizontally and spread one half with a little buttercream. Replace the top and spread the remaining buttercream over the top and sides of the cake using a palette knife to make a flat surface. Place the cake on a serving plate.

Colour half the sugarpaste lilac and half pale pink with a few spots of paste food colouring. Roll out a little pink paste thickly on a surface lightly dusted with icing sugar and stamp out 5 small hearts for the counters. Repeat with the lilac sugarpaste cutting out 3 hearts.

Take a little pink sugarpaste and roll it between your palms to make 5 thin long sausages, 25 cm/10 inches long. Roll another 5 thin lengths in lilac sugarpaste. Position the lengths on top of the cake in a grid pattern as shown in the photo, trimming the joins with scissors to neaten. Place the counters on the squares.

Roll the remaining pink and lilac sugarpaste into small balls. Press on the balls alternately round the base of the cake to make a pretty decorative border.

Forget Me Not Cake

Serves 80

1 x 30 cm/12 inch square rich fruit
cake (*see* page 27), covered in
almond paste (*see* page 56)
1 x 20 cm/8 inch square rich fruit
cake, covered in almond paste

To decorate:

2.25 kg/5 lb ready-to-roll
sugarpaste icing
blue paste food colouring
icing sugar, for dusting
$^1/_2$ batch royal icing (*see* page 46)

Place the large cake on a 40 cm/14 inch square cake drum and
the smaller square on a thin 20 cm/8 inch square board. Push
4 sticks of wooden or plastic dowelling evenly into the large cake
base, cut to the depth of the cake.

Knead 875 g/1$^3/_4$ lb white sugarpaste into a square large enough
to cover the top and sides of the 20 cm/8 inch cake. Brush the
top and sides of the almond paste with a little cold boiled water
then lift the sugarpaste over the top of the cake. Smooth the
sugarpaste down over the cake, then trim the edges neatly.
Repeat with the larger cake, then stack the smaller cake on top.

Colour the white sugarpaste trimmings bright blue and roll out
thinly on a surface lightly dusted with icing sugar. Using large
and small daisy cutters, stamp out 25 large and 25 small daisies.
Fill a piping bag fitted with a small plain nozzle with the royal
icing and pipe a small dot in the centre of each blue flower.
Leave to firm for 24 hours.

Trim round the base of each cake with a fine blue silk ribbon and
attach with a little royal icing. Pipe a small dab of royal icing
underneath each daisy and attach to the top and sides of the
cake in a flowing cascade as shown.

Gift Boxes Cake

Serves 30

For the cake base:

1 x 15 cm/6 inch square Madeira
cake (*see* page 30)
1 x 20 cm/8 inch square
Madeira cake

To decorate:

1 batch buttercream
(*see* page 38)
2 kg/4 lb ready-to-roll
sugarpaste icing
peach and cream paste
food colouring
icing sugar, for dusting

Trim the top of the cakes flat if they have peaked and spread the buttercream over the top and sides of the cakes. Place the smaller cake on a 15 cm/6 inch thin cake board and the larger one on a 25 cm/10 inch cake board. Colour 350 g/12 oz sugarpaste cream and the rest a darker peach colour. Roll out a strip of the dark peach sugarpaste wide enough to go around the sides of each cake on a surface lightly dusted with icing sugar. Stick the strips to the sides of each cake and trim the base. Roll out a square 20 cm/8 in wide and place this over the top of the smaller cake. Smooth down over the top and mould the corners smoothly. Repeat, covering the larger cake with a 25 cm/10 inch wide square.

Smooth over the tops and sides of each cake then stack the smaller on top of the larger one. Roll out the cream sugarpaste thinly and cut into strips, 3 cm/1¼ inches wide. Dampen the underside of the strips with a little cold boiled water; stick to the sides of the cake to form a flat ribbon. Take 2 short strips and trim the ends into 'V' shapes. Attach to the top cake. Take 2 short strips, fold in half and place on top of the cake. Pinch the centres together then wrap a small strip of icing over the join in the centre of the bow. Place cotton wool balls in the centres of the bowl, leave for 3 hours, then remove when firm.

Roll cream trimmings into long thin sausages with your palms, then stick the strips round the base of each cake to trim neatly.

Butterfly Cake

Serves 12–14

For the cake base:

1 x 20 cm/8 inch round Madeira
cake (*see* page 30)
3 tbsp apricot glaze

To decorate:

1.25 kg/2¹/₄ lb ready-to-roll
sugarpaste icing
icing sugar, for dusting
yellow, pink and green paste
food colouring
¹/₂ batch royal icing (*see* page 46)

Trim the top of the cake flat if it has peaked and brush the glaze over the top and sides of the cake. Knead 550 g/1¹/₄ lb sugarpaste and roll out on a surface lightly dusted with icing sugar to a circle large enough to cover the top and sides of the cake. Using both hands, carefully lift over the cake and smooth down over the top and sides. Trim the edges then place the cake on a 25 cm/10 inch cake board or flat serving plate.

Colour 75 g/3 oz sugarpaste yellow and 75 g/3 oz pink. Roll out the yellow paste thinly and cut out 2 butterfly wings using a cutter or following the pattern on page 250. Stamp out 2 small yellow daisies with daisy cutters. Repeat cutting out 3 small pink daisies. Leave on nonstick baking parchment for 2 hours to firm.

Using a sheet of nonstick baking parchment, trace out a daisy design. Mark this onto the top of the cake with a fine skewer. Colour the royal icing pale green and place in a piping bag fitted with a fine plain nozzle.

Pipe the outline of the flower pattern and butterfly wings onto the cake then fill in the shapes by flooding each one with a little royal icing. Leave to dry out for 2 hours then attach the butterfly wings and the daisies as shown with a little royal icing.

Simple Chocolate Cake

Serves 12–14

For the cake base:

1 x 20 cm/8 inch round chocolate cake (*see* page 29)

To decorate:

1 batch chocolate buttercream (*see* page 38)
1 batch chocolate covering icing (*see* page 50)
icing sugar, for dusting
125 g/4 oz ivory ready-to-roll sugarpaste icing
125 g/4 oz dark chocolate
edible silver balls

Trim the top of the cake flat if it has peaked. Spread the top and sides of the cake thinly with half the buttercream. Place the remaining buttercream in a piping bag fitted with a small star nozzle.

Knead the chocolate icing until soft then roll out on a surface lightly dusted with icing sugar to a circle large enough to cover the cake. Lift onto the cake and smooth down over the top and sides, then trim the edges neatly.

Make 3 roses from the ivory sugarpaste following the instructions on page 62. Leave to dry out in egg boxes lined with crumpled foil for 2 hours.

Break the chocolate into small pieces and melt in a heatproof bowl standing over a pan of warm water. Pour the chocolate into a small piping bag fitted with a plain nozzle. Working quickly while the chocolate is still wet, pipe spirals round the top edge of the cake.

Place the cake on a 25 cm/10 inch round board or cake plate and pipe a shell border round the base with the reserved buttercream. Decorate the cake with silver balls then place the 3 roses in the centre to finish.

Daisies Cupcakes

Makes 12

For the cakes:

1 batch vanilla cupcakes
(*see* page 32)

To decorate:

125 g/4 oz ready-to-roll
sugarpaste icing
icing sugar, for dusting
yellow gel icing tube
1 batch cream cheese frosting
(*see* page 44)
yellow paste food colouring

Roll out the sugarpaste thinly on a surface lightly dusted with icing sugar and stamp out daisy shapes with a fluted daisy cutter.

Leave these to dry out for 30 minutes on baking parchment until firm enough to handle.

Pipe a small yellow gel dot into the centre of each one. Colour the frosting pale yellow, then spread onto the cakes using a palette knife.

Press the daisies onto the frosting.

Rose Petal Cake

Serves 12–14

For the cake base:

1 x 20 cm/8 inch round Madeira
cake (*see* page 30)

To decorate:

1 medium egg white
5 fresh red roses
caster sugar, for dusting
2 tsp rose water
2 batches buttercream
(*see* page 38)

Beat the egg white with until frothy. Separate 2 of the roses into petals and brush away any dust with a clean soft brush. Do not wash the flowers.

Paint a thin layer of egg white carefully over the petals, the whole roses and rose leaves. Sprinkle each item lightly with caster sugar, then shake lightly to remove any excess. Leave on a rack lined with nonstick baking parchment for 3–4 hours until dry and sparkling.

Trim the top of the cake flat if it has peaked and place the cake on a serving plate. Beat the rose water into the buttercream to flavour it and place one quarter of it in a piping bag fitted with a star nozzle. Cut the cake in half horizontally then spread one half with a little buttercream and sandwich the other layer on top. Spread the top and sides with the remaining buttercream, pulling an icing ruler across the top to give a flat surface.

Pipe a border of stars round the top and base of the cake. Just before serving arrange the 3 large roses and leaves in the centre of the cake then scatter the top of the cake with frosted rose petals.

Spotty Chocolate Cake

Serves 8–10

For the cake base:

1 x 15 cm/6 inch round chocolate
cake (*see* page 29)
3 tbsp apricot glaze

To decorate:

700 g/1 1/2 lb ready-to-roll
sugarpaste icing
brown and red and pink paste
food colouring
icing sugar, for dusting

Trim the top of the cake flat if it has peaked and brush the glaze over the top and sides of the cake. Colour 450 g/1 lb sugarpaste light brown with a few dots of paste food colouring.

Roll the sugarpaste into a round ball and flatten out, then roll out on a surface lightly dusted with icing sugar to a circle large enough to cover the top and sides of the cake. Using both hands, carefully lift the sugarpaste over the cake and smooth down over the top and sides. Trim away the edges then place the cake on a 20 cm/8 inch cake board or flat serving plate.

Colour 175 g/6 oz sugarpaste red with a few dots of paste food colouring. Roll out a thin strip 2 cm/³/₄ inch wide, long enough to go round the base of the cake. Trim the edges of the strip straight then dampen the underside with a little cold boiled water and stick the strip round the base of the cake.

Roll out the remaining white and red icing thinly and stamp out small circles 2.5 cm/1 inch wide with a plain cutter or a clean round bottle cap. Dampen the underside of the discs then stick onto the cake, alternating the colours.

Soft Lacework Cake

Serves 12–14

For the cake base:

1 x 20 cm/8 inch round Madeira
cake (*see* page 30)
3 tbsp fine shred orange
marmalade

To decorate:

2 tbsp orange liqueur, or 2 tbsp
freshly squeezed orange juice
2 batches buttercream
(*see* page 38)

Trim the top of the cake flat if it has peaked and cut the cake in half horizontally, then spread one half with the marmalade. Sandwich the other layer on top and place on a serving plate.

Beat the orange liqueur or juice into the buttercream to flavour it. Place one third of the buttercream in a piping bag fitted with a small plain nozzle.

Using a palette knife, spread the top and sides with the remaining buttercream. To give a good finish to the top, drag an icing ruler back and forth until the surface is flat.

Pipe 'S' shaped swirls all over the top and sides of the cake with the buttercream, then pipe dots in between the swirls.

Pipe a shell border round the base of the cake to finish. Keep the cake refrigerated until ready to serve.

Orange Yellow Roses Cake

Serves 12–14

For the cake base:

1 x 20 cm/8 inch round Madeira
cake (*see* page 30)
3 tbsp apricot glaze

To decorate:

900 g/2 lb ready-to-roll
sugarpaste icing
icing sugar, for dusting
yellow and peach paste
food colouring
1 batch royal icing (*see* page 46)

Trim the top of the cake flat if it has peaked and brush the glaze over the top and sides of the cake. Knead 550 g/1¼ lb white sugaroaste into a round ball and flatten out. Roll out on a surface lightly dusted with icing sugar to a circle large enough to cover the top and sides of the cake. Using both hands, carefully lift the sugarpaste over the cake and smooth down over the top and sides. Trim away the surplus icing round the edges, then place the cake on a 25 cm/10 inch cake board or flat serving plate.

Colour 125 g/4 oz sugarpaste yellow, 125 g/4 oz peach and leave 125 g/4 oz white. Mould the yellow sugarpaste into 3 medium roses (*see* page 62). Repeat with the peach and white sugarpastes, making 3 roses with each colour. Leave all 9 roses for 2–3 hours in egg boxes lined with crumped foil until firm.

Place half the royal icing in a piping bag fitted with a small plain nozzle and pipe small dots in sets of 3 in a triangular pattern on the top and sides of the cake. Place the remaining icing in a piping bag fitted with a star nozzle and pipe a shell border round the top of the cake.

Arrange the roses on top of the cake in sets of 3 with 1 yellow, 1 peach and 1 white rose then attach them to the cake with a dab of royal icing.

Romantic Roses Cake

Serves 8–12

For the cake base:

1 x 15 cm/6 inch round Madeira
cake (*see* page 30)
3 tbsp apricot glaze

To decorate:

450 g/1 lb ready-to-roll
sugarpaste icing
pink, red and green paste
food colouring
icing sugar, for dusting
225 g/8 oz flower paste
¹/₂ batch royal icing (*see* page 46)

Trim the top of the cake flat if it has peaked and brush the glaze over the top and sides of the cake.

Colour the sugarpaste icing pale pink with a few dots of paste food colouring. Roll the icing into a ball and flatten out, then roll out on a surface lightly dusted with icing sugar to a circle large enough to cover the top and sides of the cake. Using both hands, carefully lift the sugarpaste over the cake and smooth down over the top and sides. Trim away the edges then place the cake on a 20 cm/8 inch cake board or flat serving plate.

Colour three quarters of the flower paste red and the rest green. Mould the red flower paste into 3 roses (*see* page 62) then roll out the green icing thinly, cut into leaves and mark on veins with a sharp knife. Leave the roses and leaves for 2–3 hours in egg boxes lined with crumped foil until firm.

Place the royal icing in a piping bag fitted with a small plain nozzle and pipe small dots on the top and sides of the cake. Arrange the roses and leaves on top of the cake, attaching them to the cake with a dab of royal icing. Trim the base of the cake with a strip of thin red satin ribbon and attach with a dab of royal icing.

Seasonal Fruits Cake

Serves 20

For the cake base:

1 x 20 cm/8 inch round rich fruit
cake (*see* page 26), covered
with almond paste
(*see* page 56)

To decorate:

700 g/1¹/₂ lb ready-to-roll
sugarpaste icing
icing sugar, for dusting
green, red, orange and purple
paste food colouring
caster sugar
¹/₂ batch royal icing (*see* page 46)
edible silver balls

Take 500 g/1¹/₄ lb sugarpaste and roll out on a surface lightly dusted with icing sugar to a circle large enough to cover the top and sides of the cake. Brush the almond paste with a little cold boiled water then lift the sugarpaste over the cake and smooth down over the top and sides. Trim the edges and place on a 25 cm/10 inch board or serving plate.

Colour 75 g/3 oz sugarpaste green and roll out thinly. Cut out 4 ivy shaped leaves then mark veins onto the leaves with a sharp knife.

Colour the remaining sugarpaste red and orange and a small scrap purple. Roll into small and larger balls to represent apples, oranges and grapes and coat each in caster sugar for a sparkly effect. Mark details on with a skewer.

Dampen underneath each leaf lightly with a little cold boiled water then position the leaves in the centre of the cake. Place the fruits and silver balls on the leaves attaching with a small dab of royal icing.

Fill a piping bag fitted with a small star nozzle with the royal icing and pipe a shell border round the base of the cake.

Dotty Daisy Cake

Serves 60

For the cake base:

1 x 20 cm/8 inch round Madeira
cake (*see* page 30), covered
with almond paste
(*see* page 56)
1 x 15 cm/6 inch round Madeira
cake, covered with almond paste

To decorate:

1.75 kg/3¹/₂ lb ready-to-roll
sugarpaste icing
icing sugar, for dusting
125 g/4 oz flower paste
pink and yellow paste food colouring
¹/₄ batch royal icing (*see* page 46)

Divide the sugarpaste into 700 g/1¹/₂ lb and 450 g/1 lb batches. Use the larger sugarpaste batch to cover the largest cake. Use the smaller batch to cover the smaller cake. Place the large cake on a 25 cm/10 inch round cake drum. Place the small cake on a thin 15 cm/6 inch round board. Push 4 sticks of wooden or plastic dowelling evenly into the large cake base, cut to the depth of the cake. Leave the cakes to dry out for 24 hours.

Make the spiral decorations. Take 25 g/1 oz flower paste and roll out to a very thin sausage between your palms of your hands. Cover the handle of a wooden spoon with clingfilm then wind the flower paste round the handle in a spiral pattern. Leave the spiral decoration to harden for 24 hours. Make 2 white spirals and 1 coloured pink.

Divide three quarters of the remaining sugarpaste pale pink and a quarter yellow. Roll a strip of pink sugarpaste 1 cm/¹/₂ inch wide, long enough to go round the base of the cake, then attach this with a little cold boiled water. Stack the cakes on top of each other. Roll the yellow and pink icings out thinly and stamp out small discs 2 cm/³/₄ inch wide and stick these onto the top and sides of the cake. Roll small balls of pink paste into petals and make a round yellow centre and stick to the cake with a dab of royal icing. Slip the spirals carefully out of the spoon handles then attach to the cake with a dab of royal icing.

Blue Chocolate Bow Cake

Serves 40–50

For the cake base:

2 x 20 cm/8 inch round chocolate
cakes *(see* page 29)
2 x 15 cm/6 inch round
chocolate cakes

To decorate:

1¹/₂ batches chocolate
buttercream *(see* page 38)
500 g/1 lb 2 oz almond paste
1.75 kg/3¹/₂ lb ready-to-roll
sugarpaste icing
blue paste food colouring
icing sugar, for dusting
1 batch chocolate covering icing
(see page 50)

Trim the top of the cakes flat if they have peaked. Stack the two larger cakes on top of each other and sandwich together with buttercream. Repeat with the smaller cakes. Place the smaller cake on a 15 cm/6 inch thin cake board. Coat the top and sides of each cake with buttercream. Divide the almond paste into two batches of one quarter and three quarters. Roll the almond paste into thin strips deep enough to go around the sides of each cake. Press around the sides of each cake to give a straight flat edge.

Colour the sugarpaste light blue and divide into 700 g/1¹/₂ lb and 900 g/2 lb batches. Cover each cake with sugarpaste. Roll out the blue trimmings thinly and cover the large cake board. Place the large cake on the board, then stack the smaller one on top.

Knead the chocolate covering until soft then roll out thinly and cut into long strips, 3 cm/1¹/₄ inches wide. Drape the strips over the sides of the cake and stick in place with a little cold boiled water to form a flat ribbon. Take 2 strips and trim the ends into 'V' shapes. Attach to the top cake. Take 2 short strips, fold in half and place on top of the cake in a bow shape. Pinch the centres together then wrap a small strip of icing over the join in the centre of the bow. Place cotton wool balls in the centres of the bows and leave for 3 hours, then remove when set.

Blue Orchid Cake

Serves 20–24

For the cake base:

1 x 25 cm/10 inch round Madeira
cake (*see* page 30)

To decorate:

1 batch buttercream
(*see* page 38)
900 g/2 lb ready-to-roll
sugarpaste icing
icing sugar, for dusting
225 g/8 oz flower paste
blue paste food colouring
flower stamens
¹/₂ batch royal icing (*see* page 46)
blue dusting powder

Trim the top of the cake flat if it has peaked. Cut the cake in half horizontally and spread one half with a little buttercream. Replace the top layer and spread the remaining buttercream over the top and sides of the cake.

Cover the cake with the sugarpaste. Trim the edges then place the cake on a 25 cm/10 inch cake board or flat serving plate.

Roll out the flower paste thinly and, using a large orchid cutter, cut out 5 large orchid petals. Bend the tips of the petals over and leave to firm over pieces of crumpled foil. Model a large stamen for the orchid centre. Colour a little flower paste light blue and cut out 3 light blue petals. Stamp out 5 small daisies and stick onto flower stamens, repeat making 5 white daises and leave to dry out for 3 hours.

Arrange the flower petals around the stamen centre and stick onto the cake with a dab of royal icing. Arrange the blue petals and daises around the orchid then sprinkle the centre with blue dusting powder. Tie a thin pink stain ribbon round the cake at an angle. Place the royal icing in a piping bag fitted with a small star nozzle and pipe a shell border round the base to finish.

Appliqué Flower Cake

Serves 12–14

For the cake base:

1 x 20 cm/8 inch round Madeira
cake (*see* page 30)
3 tbsp apricot glaze

To decorate:

1.25 kg/2¹/₄ lb ready-to-roll
sugarpaste icing
icing sugar, for dusting
lilac and pink paste food colouring
¹/₄ batch royal icing (*see* page 46)

Trim the top of the cake flat if it has peaked and brush the glaze over the top and sides of the cake. Knead 550 g/1¹/₄ lb white sugarpaste into a round ball and flatten out. Roll out on a surface lightly dusted with icing sugar to a circle large enough to cover the top and sides of the cake. Using both hands, carefully lift the sugarpaste over the cake and smooth down over the top and sides. Trim round the edges, then place the cake on a 25 cm/ 10 inch cake board or flat serving plate.

Colour 125 g/4 oz sugarpaste lilac and 125 g/4 oz deep pink. Roll out the lilac sugarpaste thinly and, using flower cutters, stamp out 2 large and 2 small daisy shapes, 8 small daisies, and 4 star shaped flowers. Repeat using the pink and white sugarpastes.

Dampen the underside of each flower with a little cold boiled water and stick the flowers on top and round the sides of the cake. Build up layers of petals in contrasting shades and shapes as shown in the photo. Mark details onto the flowers with a skewer.

Place the royal icing in a piping bag fitted with a small star nozzle and pipe a shell border round the base of the cake to finish.

Winter Cupcakes

Makes 12

For the cakes:

1 batch vanilla cupcakes
(*see* page 32)

To decorate:

3 tbsp apricot glaze
450 g/1 lb almond paste
225 g/8 oz ready-to-roll
sugarpaste icing
icing sugar, for dusting
1 batch royal icing (*see* page 46)

To decorate the cupcakes, trim the top of each cake level, then brush with apricot glaze.

Roll out the almond paste and cut out eight discs 6 cm/2$^{1}/_{2}$ inches wide. Place these over the glaze and press level. Leave to dry for 24 hours if possible.

Roll out the sugarpaste on a surface lightly dusted with icing sugar and stamp out holly leaf and ivy shapes, or use the patterns on page 249. Leave to dry for 2 hours on nonstick baking parchment or clingfilm.

Swirl the royal icing over the top of each cupcake. Press in the holly and ivy shapes and leave to set for 2 hours.

Cakes for Entertaining

There is nothing more important when entertaining than to provide your guests with delicious food to keep the conversation flowing, and what better way than with a cake? Whether it is an Emerald Tones Cake, perfect for a dinner party, or the tiered Lilac Cascades Cake for a larger occasion; allowing yourself to indulge in some of these fabulous cakes is a special treat that no one should deny themselves!

Buttons Ruffles Cake

Serves 20

For the cake base:

1 x 20 cm/8 inch round rich fruit cake (*see* page 26), covered in almond paste (*see* page 56)

To decorate:

1.25 kg/2¹/₂ lb ready-to-roll sugarpaste icing
blue and pink paste food colouring
icing sugar, for dusting

Colour 275 g/10 oz sugarpaste pale blue and 75 g/3 oz pale pink. Roll out the blue sugarpaste thinly on a surface lightly dusted with icing sugar and, using a button stamp, cut out 60 blue buttons. Model a large blue button. Roll out a strip of blue sugarpaste 4 cm/1¹/₂ inches wide and roll round in a spiral, then frill this out and pinch the base together. Repeat, rolling out 2 pink strips as before. Leave the buttons and ruffles to firm on a sheet of nonstick baking parchment for 2 hours.

For the ruched effect, roll out a strip of white sugarpaste thinly to an oblong, 4 cm/1¹/₂ inches wide. Starting at the base of the cake, dampen the ends of the strip with a little cold boiled water then press one end onto the cake. Pinch the end of the strip together to make a small pleat, then leaving the centre raised up, repeat and pleat the other end, pressing onto the cake.

Continue to press and pleat the strips onto the cake until you have covered the sides and top of the cake. Dampen the underside of each button and press onto the cake in the indentations between the pleats. Attach the large button and the pink and blue bows.

Colourful Chocolate Cake

Serves 12–14

For the cake base:

1 x 20 cm/8 inch round chocolate cake (*see* page 29)

To decorate:

125 g/4 oz ready-to-roll sugarpaste icing
green, pink, blue and yellow paste food colourings
icing sugar, for dusting
tube of yellow piping icing
coloured sprinkles
225 g/8 oz dark chocolate
250 ml/9 fl oz double cream
coloured sprinkles

Trim the top of the cake flat if it has peaked and cut in half horizontally.

Colour 25 g/1 oz sugarpaste green then divide the rest into 15 g/¹/₂ oz balls and colour these light pink, dark pink, blue and yellow and leave one ball white. Roll out the sugarpastes thinly on a surface lightly dusted with icing sugar and, using flower cutters, stamp out large and small daisy shapes. Pipe small yellow dots in the centres of the flowers with the tube of piping icing. Cut out small green leaves from the green sugarpaste and leave the flowers and leaves to dry for 1 hour.

Make the soft chocolate icing. Break the chocolate into pieces and melt in a heatproof bowl standing over a pan of warm water. Stir in the cream, then beat with a wooden spoon until smooth.

Cool the icing and beat again, then spread a little on one cake half. Add the other layer and sandwich the cake together. Quickly spread the chocolate icing over the top and sides of the cake with a palette knife then place the leaves and daisies in the wet icing. Scatter coloured sprinkles round the sides of the cake and leave to set. Lift the cake onto a flat plate when the icing is set and keep refrigerated until serving.

Draped Floral Cake

Serves 12–14

For the cake base:

1 x 20 cm/8 inch round Madeira
cake (*see* page 30)
3 tbsp apricot glaze

To decorate:

1.35 kg/2³/₄ lb ready-to-roll
sugarpaste icing
icing sugar, for dusting
¹/₄ batch royal icing (*see* page 46)
orange and green paste
food colouring
yellow stamens
edible silver balls

Trim the top of the cake flat if it has peaked and brush the glaze over the top and sides of the cake. Cover the cake with 550 g/1¹/₄ lb sugarpaste and place on a 25 cm/10 inch cake board or flat serving plate. Place the royal icing in a piping bag fitted with a star nozzle and pipe a shell border round the base.

Colour 350 g/12 oz sugarpaste orange and 125 g/4 oz green. Roll out the orange sugarpaste thinly and cut out flat oval shapes with a petal cutter. Wrap a petal around a yellow stamen, then wrap another petal around this. Continue wrapping 6–7 petals around each flower then pinch the base together and pull away excess icing to neaten. Place in an egg box lined with crumpled foil, flicking out the petals, and leave for 4 hours until firm. Make 3 large and 9 smaller flowers. Roll out the green icing and cut out 10 green leaves with a cutter. Roll each leaf round to curl it, then leave to dry and harden.

Roll 225 g/8 oz white sugarpaste thinly to an oblong, 13 cm/5 inches x 30 cm/12 inches. Lightly brush the front of the cake with a little cold water then attach the sugarpaste, draping it in folds as shown. Press the top and base ends firmly to stick to the cake. Arrange the flowers and leaves over the top join in a cascade and stick on with a dab of royal icing. Attach a single flower and leaf on the base join. Finish the top of the cake with edible silver balls.

Cherry Blossom Cake

Serves 12–14

For the cake base:

1 x 20 cm/8 inch round Madeira
cake (*see* page 30)
3 tbsp apricot glaze

To decorate:

1.25 kg/2¹/₂ lb ready-to-roll
sugarpaste icing
icing sugar, for dusting
pink and brown paste food colouring
edible silver balls
¹/₄ batch royal icing (*see* page 46)

Trim the top of the cake flat if it has peaked and brush the glaze over the top and sides of the cake. Cover the cake with 550 g/1¹/₄ lb white sugarpaste. Trim away the edges, then place the cake on a 25 cm/10 inch cake board or flat serving plate.

Colour 125 g/4 oz sugarpaste pale pink and roll out thinly. Using daisy cutters, stamp out 20 small and 20 larger daisy shapes. Press a silver ball in the centre of each flower. Leave to dry for 1 hour to harden.

Colour the royal icing dark brown and place in a piping bag fitted with a small plain nozzle. Pipe on the outline of a tree trunk with branches, following the photo. Fill in the outline with the brown icing and while the icing is still wet, attach the pink flowers to the branches, placing the smaller ones at the ends. Leave to dry for 1 hour then attach a narrow brown satin ribbon round the base to finish.

Blue Lacework Cake

Serves 15–20

For the cake base:

1 x 15 cm/6 inch round rich fruit
cake (see page 26), covered in
almond paste (see page 56)

To decorate:

450 g/1 lb ready-to-roll sugarpaste
pale blue paste food colouring
icing sugar, for dusting
1 batch royal icing (see page 46)
75 g/3 oz white sugarpaste roses
(see page 62)

Colour the sugarpaste pale blue with paste food colouring and
use to cover the cake. Trim away the edges.

Place the cake on a 20 cm/8 inch round board and attach a net
frill round the base. Place one quarter of the royal icing in a
piping bag fitted with a small plain nozzle and pipe a border of
small dots round the base of the cake.

Trace star flower shapes (see page 252) as a guide onto the
sides of the cake with a small skewer. Fill a piping bag fitted
with a small plain nozzle with the remaining royal icing.

Pipe a thin line round the outline of the petals then take a fine
paintbrush and dampen the tip with a little cold boiled water.
Use the brush to drag the icing from the outside of the outline
into the middle of the flower. Pipe a small circlet of dots in the
centre of each flower. Repeat, covering the sides of the cake.
Pipe swags in small dotted lines on the top edge of the cake

Attach the white roses on top of the cake with a dab of royal
icing and leave the icing to dry out for 5 hours.

Rosemary Cranberry Cupcakes

Makes 12

For the cakes:

1 batch vanilla cupcakes
(*see* page 32)

To decorate:

1 egg white
12 small rosemary sprigs
125 g/4 oz fresh red cranberries
caster sugar, for dusting
3 tbsp apricot glaze
350 g/12 oz ready-to-roll
sugarpaste icing
icing sugar, for dusting

Place a sheet of nonstick baking parchment on a flat surface.

Beat the egg white until frothy, then brush thinly over the rosemary and cranberries and place them on the nonstick baking parchment. Dust with caster sugar and leave to dry out for 2–4 hours until crisp.

Brush the top of each cake with a little apricot glaze.

Roll out the sugarpaste on a surface dusted with icing sugar and cut out 12 circles 6 cm/2^1/$_2$ inches wide. Place a disc on top of each and press level.

Decorate each one with sparkly rosemary sprigs and cranberries.

Lilac Cascades Cake

Serves 60

For the cake base:

1 x 20 cm/8 inch round Madeira cake (*see* page 30), covered with almond paste (*see* page 56)
1 x 15 cm/6 inch round rich fruit cake (*see* page 26), covered with almond paste

To decorate:

1.25 kg/2 lb 8 oz ready-to-roll sugarpaste icing
icing sugar, for dusting
450 g/1 lb flower paste
purple paste food colouring
1/2 batch royal icing (*see* page 46)

Divide the sugarpaste into 550 g/1¹/₄ lb and 450 g/1 lb batches. Cover the larger cake with the larger sugarpaste batch. Repeat with the smaller cake.

Cover a 30 cm/12 inch round cake drum with the remaining sugarpaste and place the large cake on top. Place the small cake on a thin 15 cm/6 inch round board. Push 4 sticks of dowelling evenly into the large cake base, cut to the depth of the cake. Leave the cakes to dry out for 24 hours.

Colour the flower paste purple and wrap tightly in clingfilm. Roll out a little of the paste thinly and, using an open Tudor rose cutter, stamp out sets of petals and flute up the edges to curl them. Leave the petals in egg boxes lined with crumpled foil to harden for 3 hours. Make centres for the roses with a smaller cutter, repeating the process, sticking the petals together with a small dab of royal icing. Make 10 large layered flowers and 50 small open flowers.

Stack the cakes on top of each other and trim round the base with a satin ribbon. Stick the flowers to the cake with small dabs of royal icing, arranging them over the top, sides and round the base of the cake.

Pink Band Cake

Serves 60

For the cake base:

1 x 15 cm/6 inch round Madeira
cake (*see* page 30)
1 x 25 cm/10 inch round
Madeira cake

To decorate:

1¹/₂ batches buttercream
(*see* page 38)
1.75 kg/3¹/₂ lb ready-to-roll
sugarpaste icing
pink and yellow paste
food colouring
icing sugar, for dusting
1 batch royal icing (*see* page 46)

Trim the top of the cakes and spread the top and sides with buttercream. Colour 1.25 kg/2¹/₂ lb sugarpaste light pink with a little paste food colouring. Cover the larger cake with 700 g/1¹/₂ lb pink sugarpaste. Repeat with the smaller cake. Place the large cake on a 25 cm/10 inch cake board and the small one on a thin 15 cm/6 inch round board.

Colour pink trimmings a darker pink with paste food colouring. Roll out thinly and, using a large daisy flower cutter, stamp out 16 large daisy shapes. Leave to dry out on nonstick baking parchment. Colour the royal icing pale cream and place half in a piping bag fitted with a small plain nozzle. Pipe a small dot in the centre of each daisy. Colour a little royal icing yellow and pipe thin lines spaced well apart round the sides of each cake.

Roll out 450 g/1 lb white sugarpaste thinly. Using a 7.5 cm/3 inch plain round cutter, cut out 16 discs. Using a 4 cm/1½ inch cutter, cut out a smaller disc from the centre of each one. Fold the 'O' shape over into 2 loops, one higher than the other and pinch the ends. Dampen each end of the loop and press onto the top edge of the large cake. Continue making and attaching 10 loops around the large cake and 6 loops round the small cake. Attach a daisy in between each swag with a blob of royal icing. Stack the cakes. Place the remaining royal icing in a piping bag with a small star nozzle and pipe a shell border round the cake bases.

Summer Garland Cake

Serves 12–14

For the cake base:

1 x 20 cm/8 inch round Madeira
cake (*see* page 30)

To decorate:

2 batches buttercream
(*see* page 38)
orange and lilac paste
food colouring
125 g/4 oz ready-to-roll
sugarpaste icing
icing sugar, for dusting
dolly mixture sweets

Trim the top of the cake flat if it has peaked and place the cake on a serving plate. Cut the cake in half horizontally, then spread one half with a little buttercream. Sandwich the other layer on top and place on a serving plate.

Colour one third of the remaining buttercream light orange and place in a piping bag fitted with a small star nozzle. Using a palette knife, spread the top and sides with the remaining buttercream.

Colour the sugarpaste lilac and roll out thinly on a surface lightly dusted with icing sugar. Stamp out 6 large daisies with a daisy cutter.

Pipe a thick rope border round the top of the cake with the orange buttercream then place the daisies on this, equally spaced apart. Fill the centre of each daisy with a piped star. Scatter the sweets on the border in between the daisies. Pipe a shell border round the base of the cake to finish. Keep the cake refrigerated until ready to serve.

Bluebird Cupcakes

Makes 12

For the cakes:

1 batch vanilla cupcakes
(*see* page 32)

To decorate:

125 g/4 oz ready-to-roll
sugarpaste icing
blue paste food colouring
icing sugar, for dusting
1 batch cream cheese frosting
(*see* page 44)
white gel icing tube

To decorate the cupcakes, colour the sugarpaste blue.

Roll out the sugarpaste thinly on a surface lightly dusted with icing sugar and mark out bird wings in sets of two and one body per bird.

Trace round the patterns on page 250 and mark them onto the icing, then stamp out some daisy shapes. Leave all these to dry out on nonstick baking parchment for 30 minutes until firm enough to handle.

Swirl the frosting onto each cupcake. Press one bird's body and pair of wings, and some flowers, onto the frosting and pipe on decorations with the white gel icing.

A Rose Garden Cake

Serves 12–14

For the cake base:

1 x 20 cm/8 inch round Madeira
cake (*see* page 30)
3 tbsp apricot glaze

To decorate:

900 g/2 lb almond paste
green and orange paste
food colouring
¹/₄ batch royal icing (*see* page 46)

Trim the top of the cake flat if it has peaked and brush the glaze over the top and sides of the cake. Roll out 450 g/1 lb almond paste and use to cover the top of the cake, then trim away the surplus round the edges.

Colour 225 g/8 oz almond paste emerald green. Divide in half and roll one half out to a strip long enough to go round the sides of the cake. Press onto the sides of the cake and trim neatly.

Roll the remaining green almond paste out thinly and cut out 16 large leaves, 8 smaller leaves and a thin stem shape. Mark veins on the leaves with a sharp knife and curl up the edges slightly. Colour the remaining almond paste peach and model into 5 roses, the same as you would with sugarpaste (*see* page 62). Place the leaves and roses on the cake securing with a small dab of royal icing.

Colour half the royal icing peach and place in a piping bag fitted with a small plain nozzle. Place the remaining white icing in a separate bag fitted with a small plain nozzle. Pipe small dots alternating white and peach colours round the top edge of the cake to make a neat border. Place the cake on a 25 cm/10 inch cake board or flat plate to serve.

Elegant Lilies Cake

Serves 15–20

For the cake base:

1 x 15 cm/6 inch round rich fruit cake (*see* page 26), covered with almond paste (*see* page 56)

To decorate:

900 g/2 lb ready-to-roll sugarpaste icing
yellow and peach paste food colouring
icing sugar, for dusting
¹/₂ batch royal icing (*see* page 46)

Cover the cake with 450 g/1 lb sugarpaste.

Colour 50 g/2 oz sugarpaste light peach and roll out thinly on a surface lightly dusted with icing sugar. Stamp out 20 small daisies with a flower cutter. Using white sugarpaste, repeat, stamping out 20 white daisies. Leave the flowers to dry on a sheet of nonstick baking parchment.

Following the instructions on page 63, make 15 small lilies, colouring 75 g/3 oz sugarpaste yellow for the centres and using the remaining white sugarpaste for the petals. Leave for 2–3 hours.

Cover the cake with the remaining sugarpaste, trim and place on a 20 cm/8 inch round base. Place the royal icing in a piping bag fitted with a small plain nozzle and pipe a border of small dots round the base of the cake.

Using small dabs of icing, attach the daisies round the sides of the cake. Make a small ball with sugarpaste trimmings and place on top of the cake. Arrange the lilies round this as shown.

Emerald Tones Cake

Serves 18

For the cake base:

1 x 20 cm/8 inch square chocolate
cake (*see* page 29)

To decorate:

¹/₂ batch buttercream (*see* page 38)
1.35 kg/2³/₄ lb ready-to-roll
sugarpaste icing
icing sugar, for dusting
green paste food colouring

Trim the top of the cake flat if it has peaked, cut the cake in half
horizontally and spread with a little buttercream, then spread the
remainder over the top and sides of the cake.

Cover the cake with 550 g/1¹/₄ lb white sugarpaste. Trim round the
edges, then place the cake on a 25 cm/10 inch cake board or flat
serving plate.

Divide the remaining sugarpaste in half. Keep one half white and
colour the other half in three batches of dark, medium and light
green. Starting with the dark green paste, roll a small thin strip,
1 cm/¹/₂ inches wide x 4 cm/1¹/₂ inches long. Roll the strip up in a
loose spiral, dampen one end with a little cold boiled water then
press onto the side of the cake.

Continue adding the spirals, making a dark double layer all
around the base of the cake. Add another double layer of medium
green spirals on top for the dark green, then a double light green
layer on top of this.

Complete the cake with a layer of white spirals across the top
edge and over the top of the cake. Add an emerald green satin
ribbon and bow to complete the cake.

Rose Garland Cake

Serves 12–14

For the cake base:

1 x 20 cm/8 inch round Madeira
cake (*see* page 30)
4 tbsp lemon curd

To decorate:

1 batch royal icing (*see* page 46)
pink, blue, yellow and green paste
food colouring
1¹/₂ batches buttercream
(*see* page 38)
coloured sprinkles

Colour the royal icing in small batches of light and dark pink, blue, yellow and green. Place a coloured batch in a small piping bag fitted with a flower petal piping nozzle. Place a small square of waxed paper on an icing nail and pipe a central dot. Pipe petals round this to make a rose. Pipe 6 light pink and 6 dark pink roses on squares of waxed paper and leave to dry out.

Pipe 6 blue daisies onto squares and finish each with a yellow dot. Pipe 24 small green leaves onto waxed paper with a small flat nozzle. Leave the flowers to dry out for 24 hours then peel away from the waxed papers.

Trim the top of the cake flat if it has peaked and cut the cake in half horizontally. Spread the lemon curd over the one cake then place the other layer back on top. Place the cake on a 25 cm/10 inch cake board or flat serving plate. Spread the buttercream thickly over the top and sides of the cake, smoothing the top of the cake flat with an icing ruler.

Arrange the flowers around the outer edge of the cake then place the leaves in between them. Scatter coloured sprinkles round the cake just before serving.

Peach Rose Cake

Serves 80–100

For the cake base:

1 x 15 cm/6 inch round rich fruit cake (*see* page 26), covered in almond paste (*see* page 56)
1 x 20 cm/8 inch round rich fruit cake, covered in almond paste
1 x 25 cm/10 inch round rich fruit cake (*see* page 27), covered in almond paste

To decorate:

2 kg/4¹/₂ lb ready-to-roll sugarpaste icing
icing sugar, for dusting
peach and pink paste food colourings
450 g/1 lb flower paste
cornflour, for dusting
¹/₂ batch royal icing (*see* page 46)

Divide the sugarpaste into 1 kg/2 lb, 750 g/1¹/₂ lb and 450 g/1 lb batches and use to cover all 3 cakes. Gather up the trimmings and the remaining sugarpaste and colour peach. Place the large cake on a 40 cm/14 inch round cake drum. Place the medium cake on a thin 20 cm/8 inch round board and the small cake on a thin 15 cm/6 inch cake board. Push 4 sticks of wooden or plastic dowelling evenly into the large cake base, cut to the depth of the cake. Repeat with the medium cake. Stack the cakes on top of each other.

Colour the flower paste pale pink and roll out very thinly on a surface lightly dusted with cornflour. Using a Tudor rose flower cutter, stamp out 40 roses. Curl the petals up into a cup shape and leave to dry out in egg boxes lined with crumpled foil until firm. Place the royal icing in a piping bag fitted with a small plain nozzle and pipe a white centre on each rose.

Roll the peach sugarpaste into thin narrow strips long enough to go round the base of each cake. Dampen the underside of each and stick to the base of each cake. Place a dab or royal icing on each rose and arrange in a cascade from the top, flowing round the sides of the cake.

Shocking Pink Party Cake

Serves 12–14

For the cake base:

1 x 20 cm/8 inch round Madeira cake (*see* page 30)

To decorate:

¹/₂ batch buttercream (*see* page 38)
pink, yellow, blue, orange, purple and green paste food colouring
900 g/2 lb ready-to-roll sugarpaste icing
icing sugar, for dusting
1 tube yellow and 1 tube green piping icing
edible silver balls

Trim the top of the cake flat if it has peaked and cut the cake in half horizontally. Spread a little buttercream over one half then sandwich the other layer on top. Spread the remaining buttercream over the top and sides of the cake.

Knead bright pink paste food colouring into 550 g/1¹/₄ lb sugarpaste, then use to cover the cake. Trim round the edges then place the cake on a 25 cm/10 inch cake board or flat serving plate.

Roll out 50 g/2 oz white sugarpaste on a surface lightly dusted with icing sugar and stamp out 4 large daisies using a fine daisy cutter. Leave the daisies to dry for 2–3 hours on nonstick baking parchment.

Colour the remaining sugarpaste in small batches of yellow, blue, orange, purple and green. Roll out the sugarpaste thinly and, using flower cutters, stamp out 12 medium daisy shapes, five small daisies and 6 green leaves. Leave to dry out for 2 hours to firm then pipe yellow centres in the flowers. Pipe a thin green spiral pattern on top of the cake, then attach the flowers on the top and round the sides of the cake with dabs of icing, then attach the silver balls.

Chocolate Boxes Cake

Serves 20

For the cake base:

1 x 13 cm/5 inch square chocolate cake (*see* page 29)
1 x 18 cm/7 inch square chocolate cake

To decorate:

1 batch chocolate buttercream (*see* page 38)
225 g/8 oz dark chocolate
225 g/8 oz white chocolate
1/2 batch chocolate modelling icing, using dark plain chocolate (*see* page 48)

Trim the top of the cakes and spread the buttercream over the top and sides of each cake. Place the small cake on a 13 cm/5 inch square thin cake board and the larger one on an 18 cm/7 inch square board.

Melt the plain and white chocolate in separate bowls. Using a palette knife, thinly spread the chocolate out on separate sheets of nonstick baking parchment. Leave until cold and set hard then, using a sharp knife, cut two squares from the white chocolate large enough to cover the tops of both cakes. Cut thin strips about 2 cm/3/4 inch wide, and the depth of the cake. Lift the strips up carefully off the paper with a small palette knife and press onto the buttercream, using alternate white and dark strips.

Place the smaller cake on top of the larger one at an angle. Melt the rest of the dark chocolate, place in a small piping bag with a plain nozzle and pipe a shell border around the top and base edges of both cakes.

Knead the modelling chocolate lightly until softened. On a surface lightly dusted with icing sugar, thinly roll to a narrow strip, 1 cm/1/2 inches wide. Cut into 14 cm/51/2 inch lengths and pinch the ends together to make loops. Place the loops around spoon handles lined with clingfilm and leave until firm. Place on top of the cake and secure with a little piped melted chocolate.

Afternoon Tea Cake

Serves 40

For the cake base:

1 x 20 cm/8 inch round Madeira
cake (*see* page 30), covered in
almond paste (*see* page 56)
1 x 15 cm/6 inch round Madeira
cake, covered in almond paste

To decorate:

1.75 kg/3¹/₂ lb ready-to-roll
sugarpaste icing
icing sugar, for dusting
pink, blue, yellow and green paste
food colouring
¹/₂ batch royal icing (*see* page 46)
edible silver balls

Cut off 450 g/1 lb sugarpaste and set aside. Divide the remaining sugarpaste into 550 g/1¹/₄ lb and 500 g/1 lb 2 oz batches. Cover the larger cake with the large sugarpaste batch. Trim the edges then repeat to cover the smaller cake.

Place the large cake on a 30 cm/12 inch cake drum and the smaller one on a 15 cm/6 inch thin round cake board. Stack the cakes using dowelling (*see* page 58).

Colour the remaining sugarpaste in small batches of light and dark pink, blue, yellow and green. Model open roses with the coloured sugarpaste (*see* page 62) and place in empty egg boxes lined with crumpled foil. Cut out small green leaves and mark on veins with a sharp knife. Leave the roses and leaves to harden for 4 hours.

Colour the royal icing pale pink and pipe a shell border round the base of each cake. Position the flowers on top and round the side of the cake and place the leaves under the flowers. Stick the flowers in place with a dab of royal icing then press the silver balls on top of each cake to finish.

In The Pink Cake

Serves 90

For the cake base:

1 x 13 cm/5 inch Madeira cake
(*see* page 30), covered in
almond paste (*see* page 56)
1 x 18 cm/7 inch chocolate cake
(*see* page 29), covered in
almond paste
1 x 25 cm/10 inch rich fruit cake
(*see* page 27), covered in
almond paste

To decorate:

2.25 kg/5 lb ready-to-roll
sugarpaste icing
pink paste food colouring
1 batch royal icing (*see* page 46)
edible silver or pearl balls
icing sugar, for dusting

Divide the sugarpaste into three and colour 450 g/1 lb pale pink, 700 g/ 1½ lb medium pink and 1.25 kg/2¼ lb dark pink. Divide the royal icing into three batches and colour these to tone with the sugarpaste. Cover the small cake with the pale pink sugarpaste. Trim the edges, then place the cake on a thin 15 cm/6 inch square board. Repeat with the medium pink sugarpaste, placing the cake on a 20 cm/8 inch thin board. Repeat with the large cake and the darker pink icing, placing the cake on a 30 cm/12 inch square cake board. Press the silver or pearl edible balls into the top and sides of the cake while the sugarpaste is still soft.

Stack the cakes on top of each other using dowelling. Place the royal icing in three small paper icing bags fitted with small star nozzles and pipe a shell border in a matching tone, round the base of each cake.

Colour the trimmings and the remaining sugarpaste medium pink with a little paste food colouring. Roll out the sugarpaste thinly on a surface lightly dusted with icing sugar and cut into strips, 4 cm/1½ inches wide. Stick strips over the sides of the cakes with a little cold boiled water to form a flat ribbon. Take 4 short strips and trim the ends. Attach to the top cake. Take the 4 short strips, fold in half and place on top of the cake. Pinch the centres together, then wrap a small strip of icing over the join in the centre of the bow. Place cotton wool balls in the centres of the bows until firm, then remove when set.

Butterfly Cupcakes

Makes 12

For the cakes:

1 batch vanilla cupcakes
(*see* page 32)

To decorate:

350 g/12 oz ready-to-roll
sugarpaste icing
lilac, blue, pink yellow paste
food colourings
icing sugar, for dusting
1 batch cream cheese frosting
(*see* page 44)
gel icing tubes
edible coloured balls

To decorate, colour the sugarpaste in batches of lilac, blue, pink and yellow.

Roll out the sugarpaste thinly on a surface lightly dusted with icing sugar and mark out daisy shapes and butterfly wings following the pattern on page 250. Leave these to dry for 30 minutes on baking parchment until firm enough to handle.

Place the frosting in a piping bag fitted with a star nozzle and pipe swirls onto each cupcake.

Press the wings and flowers onto the frosting and pipe on decorations with small gel icing. Add the coloured balls to finish.

Ribbons Bows Cake

Serves 50

For the cake base:

1 x 20 cm/8 inch round chocolate cake (*see* page 29)
1 x 25 cm/10 inch round chocolate cake

To decorate:

1¹/₂ batches buttercream (*see* page 38)
pink paste food colouring
2 kg/4 lb ready-to-roll sugarpaste icing
icing sugar, for dusting
1 batch chocolate covering icing (*see* page 50)

Trim the tops from the cakes flat if they have peaked. Colour the buttercream light pink. Cut both cakes in half horizontally and spread with a little buttercream then replace the tops and spread buttercream over the top and sides of each cake. Colour the sugarpaste pale pink. Cover the smaller cake with 550 g/1¼ lb sugarpaste. Roll out 900 g/2 lb sugarpaste and repeat to cover the larger cake. Roll out the chocolate icing to make 2 strips, 3 cm/1¼ inches wide, long enough to go round the base of each cake. Cut the edges of the strips straight with a sharp knife and press round the base of each cake. Roll the scraps out thinly and cut out twenty 2.5 cm/1 inch wide discs with a small plain cutter or a clean bottle cap. Dampen the underside of each disc with a little cold boiled water then stick them onto the sides of the cake. Stack the cakes using dowelling (*see* page 58).

Use the remaining pink sugarpaste and trimmings to make bows. Roll out thinly on a surface lightly dusted with icing sugar and cut into strips, 6 cm/2½ inches wide. Take 2 short strips and trim the ends into 'V' shapes. Attach to the top cake. Repeat and place 2 strips in front and at either side of the large cake. Take 2 short strips, fold in half and place on top of the cake. Pinch the centres together then wrap a small strip of icing over the join in the centre of the bow. Repeat making 3 bows for the large cake. Place cotton wool balls in the centres of the bows, for 3 hours, then remove when set.

Special

Occasion

Cakes

What better way to celebrate a special occasion than with a custom decorated cake that will make any occasion go with a bang! Halloween would not be complete without a Spooky Ghosts Cake, while a Party Parcels Cake will make a fun addition to any birthday. Let your romantic side shine through with an Entwined Valentine's Cake or why not have a go at making your very own wedding cake.

Mother's Day Bouquet Cake

Serves 12–14

For the cake base:

1 x 20 cm/8 inch round Madeira
cake (*see* page 30)
3 tbsp sieved apricot jam

To decorate:

1.25 kg/2¼ lb ready-to-roll
sugarpaste icing
icing sugar, for dusting
pink and green paste food colours

Trim the top of the cake flat if it has peaked and brush the jam over the top and sides of the cake. Cover the cake with 550 g/1¼ lb sugarpaste and place on a 25 cm/10 inch cake board or flat serving plate.

Colour 350 g/12 oz sugarpaste pink and 125 g/4 oz green. Roll 175 g/6 oz pink sugarpaste out on a surface lightly dusted with icing sugar to a long thin strip, 5 cm/2 inches wide x 68.5 cm/27 inches long. Dampen the underside of the ribbon by lightly brushing with a little cold boiled water. Roll the strip carefully round the outside of the cake and press the join to neaten. Keep the join at the back of the cake.

Model the remaining pink sugarpaste into 8 roses (*see* page 62) and leave these for 2–3 hours in egg boxes lined with crumped foil until firm.

Using the green sugarpaste, cut out 10 leaves and mark veins on them using a sharp knife. Roll scraps of green sugarpaste into long thin sausages. Lightly dampen the underside of the roses and leaves and arrange at the back of the cake in a semi-circle with the leaves and green stems.

Fortieth Birthday Cupcakes

Makes 12

For the cakes:

1 batch lemon cupcakes
(*see* page 32)

To decorate:

¼ batch lemon buttercream
(*see* page 38)
700 g/1½ lb ready-to-roll
sugarpaste icing
lilac paste food colouring
icing sugar, for dusting

Trim the top of each cake flat if they have peaked. Spread the top of each cake with a little buttercream.

Colour half the sugarpaste pale lilac with a few spots of paste food colouring. Roll out 225 g/8 oz white sugarpaste thinly on a surface lightly dusted with icing sugar.

Cut out six circles 6 cm/2½ inches wide with a plain round cutter or use the template on page 251. Place a disc on top of six cupcakes and press level. Repeat with the same amount of lilac sugarpaste.

Gather up the scraps and roll out with the remaining sugarpaste in one batch of white and one lilac. Using small number cutters, or the templates on page 253, cut out six white and six lilac '40' numbers.

Lightly brush the underside of the numbers with a little cold boiled water and stick the white numbers onto the lilac backgrounds and the lilac numbers onto the white backgrounds.

Using a small daisy stamper, stamp out 24 white and 24 lilac daisies. Place 4 daisies of contrasting colour on each cupcake as shown.

Party Balloons Cupcakes

Makes 12

For the cakes:

1 batch chocolate cupcakes
(*see* page 32)

To decorate:

250 g/9 oz ready-to-roll
sugarpaste icing
yellow, red and blue paste
food colouring
36 small soft fruit jelly sweets
1 batch thick glacé icing
(*see* page 54)
small tube of black piping icing

Trim the top of each cake flat if they have peaked.

Divide the sugarpaste into three and colour each batch yellow, red and blue. Take enough sugarpaste to roll around a jelly sweet to cover.

Press out into an oval shape and pinch the end to make a small ridge. Make 12 yellow, 12 blue and 12 red small balloons.

Make the glacé icing to a thick coating consistency and then spread 2–3 teaspoons on top of each cake to cover.

Press one yellow, one red and one blue balloon into the wet icing and leave to firm for about 1 hour.

When the white icing is set, pipe on thin strings and a bow with black piping icing. Repeat with the remaining cakes.

Party Parcels Cake

Serves 12–14

For the cake base:

1 x 20 cm/8 inch round chocolate
cake (*see* page 29)

To decorate:

$^1/_2$ batch buttercream (*see* page 38)
1.3 kg/1 lb 12 oz ready-to-roll
sugarpaste icing
icing sugar, for dusting
blue, red, yellow and green paste
food colouring
shop-bought tubes of green, yellow,
red and white piping icing or
$^1/_2$ batch royal icing (*see* page 46)
, coloured in batches and placed in
small piping bags with small
plain nozzles

Trim the top of the cake flat if it has peaked and cut the cake in half horizontally. Spread one half with one quarter of the buttercream, replace the top layer, then spread the remaining buttercream thinly over the top and sides of the cake.

Knead 550 g/1$^1/_4$ lb white sugarpaste into a ball and flatten out. Roll out on a surface lightly dusted with icing sugar to a circle large enough to cover the top and sides of the cake. Using both hands, carefully lift the sugarpaste over the cake and smooth down over the top and sides. Trim away the edges then place the cake on a 25 cm/10 inch cake board or flat serving plate.

Colour 50 g/2 oz batches of sugarpaste blue, red, yellow and green. Roll out each colour thinly and cut into neat squares and oblongs with a sharp knife.

Dampen the underside of each square with a little cold boiled water then stick the parcels onto the cake in a random pattern.

Pipe ribbons and bows on the parcels in a contrasting colour, piping patterns and dots on each square to decorate.

Giftwrapped Cake

*

Serves 20

For the cake base:

1 x 20 cm/8 inch square Madeira
cake (*see* page 30)
6 tbsp apricot glaze

To decorate:

1.25 kg/2$^1/_2$ lb ready-to-roll
sugarpaste icing
icing sugar, for dusting
royal blue and pale blue paste
food colouring

Trim the top of the cake if it has peaked. Spread the apricot glaze over the top and sides of the cake. Cover the cake with 700 g/1$^1/_2$ lb sugarpaste and place on a 25 cm/10 inch cake board.

Colour two thirds of the remaining icing royal blue; and one third in two batches, one mid blue and one pale blue. Roll out the royal blue icing to a long thin strip and cut out 3 ribbon strips, 36 cm/14 inches long x 4 cm/1$^1/_2$ inches wide. Re-roll the icing and cut out 4 thin strips, 50 cm/20 inchs x 2 cm/$^3/_4$ inch. Roll out the lighter blue icing and stamp out large and small discs with cutters. Use scraps of royal blue icing to cut out more discs. Brush the underside of each disc with a cold little boiled water and stick the discs onto the top and sides of the cake.

Lightly brush the underside of each ribbon with cold boiled water then stick 2 thicker ribbons over the cake as shown. Using the remaining thick ribbon, form 2 loops with short pieces together to make a bow, then trail 2 strips over the cake, fluting up the ends. Neaten the join in the centre with a scrap of blue sugarpaste.

Take one thin strip and pleat together. Brush round the base of the cake with a little cold boiled water and stick the pleated strip onto the side of the cake. Repeat with the remaining 3 strips.

Prize Rosette Cupcake

Makes 12

For the cakes:

1 batch vanilla cupcakes
(*see* page 32)

To decorate:

1 batch buttercream (*see* page 38)
600 g/1 lb 4 oz ready-to-roll
sugarpaste icing
red, yellow and blue paste
food colourings
icing sugar, for dusting
gel writing icing tubes

Trim the tops of the cakes flat if they have formed peaks. Spread buttercream over the cupcakes and set aside.

Divide the sugarpaste into three batches and colour each a different colour. Roll out the sugarpaste on a surface lightly dusted with icing sugar and stamp out a fluted circle 6 cm/2$\frac{1}{2}$ inches wide with a pastry cutter.

Out of the centre of this circle, cut away a small plain disc 3 cm/ 1¼ inches wide and discard.

Take a cocktail stick and roll this back and forth in the sugarpaste icing until it begins to frill up. Take the frilled circle and place in the buttercream, fluting up the edges.

Make another fluted circle in a contrasting colour and place this inside the first layer. Stamp out a plain circle and place this in the centre. Write prizes, such as '1st', '2nd' and 3rd', in gel icing in the centres.

Sparkly Snowflakes Cake

Serves 20

For the cake base:

1 x 20 cm/8 inch round rich fruit cake (*see* page 26), covered in almond paste (*see* page 56)

To decorate:

700 g/1½ lb ready-to-roll sugarpaste icing
pale pink paste food colouring
icing sugar, for dusting
½ batch royal icing (*see* page 46)
edible silver balls

Weigh 550 g/1¼ lb sugarpaste and colour pale pink with just a hint of pink paste food colouring. Brush the almond paste with a little cold boiled water, then cover the cake with the sugarpaste. Trim away the edges and place on a 25 cm/10 inch board or serving plate.

Roll the remaining white sugarpaste out thinly on a surface lightly dusted with icing sugar. Using a snowflake cutter, stamp out about 50 small snowflake patterns. Lift each snowflake carefully onto a sheet of nonstick baking parchment with a palette knife and leave to firm for 2 hours.

Dab the underside of each snowflake with royal icing and stick them to the top and sides of the cake. Place the remaining royal icing in a bag fitted with a small plain nozzle and pipe small dots over the cake in between the snowflakes. Press on edible silver balls to finish.

Frosty Friends Cake

Serves 20

For the cake base:

1 x 20 cm/8 inch round rich fruit
cake (*see* page 26),
covered with almond paste
(*see* page 56)

To decorate:

lilac, pink, blue, yellow,
red, green, black and orange
paste food colouring
8 plain or shortbread biscuit
rounds, 6 cm/2¹/₄ inches wide
1.25 kg/2¹/₄ lb ready-to-roll
sugarpaste icing
icing sugar, for dusting
1 batch royal icing (*see* page 46)

Brush a little cold boiled water over the almond paste then cover the cake with 550 g/1¹/₄ lb sugarpaste. Trim away the edges and reserve the trimmings, then place the cake on a 25 cm/10 inch board or serving plate. Roll 225 g/8 oz sugarpaste and into eight 50 g/2 oz balls. Colour 50 g/2 oz batches of sugarpaste in lilac, pink, blue, yellow, red and green.

Spread each biscuit thinly with a little royal icing then roll out the white balls to discs large enough to cover the biscuits. Smooth the sugarpaste over the biscuits tucking the ends underneath then roll the top flat. Mould each coloured batch, plus two white into a hat and scarf shape and stick the hats onto the snowmen's heads then make ridges with a skewer to represent woolly patterns. Colour scraps black and orange and make tiny eyes and carrot noses and stick onto the faces. Mark on a smiling mouth with a skewer.

Place one third of the royal icing in a piping bag fitted with a medium plain nozzle. Spread the remainder of the royal icing thickly round the board and base of the cake, flicking up in swirls with a small palette knife to represent snow. Place the snowmen round the base of the cake at intervals, then stick a scarf and pom pom on each head. Pipe small dots of royal icing all over the top and sides of the cake to finish.

Holly Christmas Cake

Serves 20

For the cake base:

1 x 20 cm/8 inch round rich fruit cake (*see* page 26), covered with almond paste (*see* page 56)

To decorate:

700 g/1¹/₂ lb ready-to-roll sugarpaste icing
icing sugar, for dusting
green and red paste food colouring

Weigh 550 g/1¹/₄ lb sugarpaste and roll out on a surface lightly dusted with icing sugar to a circle large enough to cover the top and sides of the cake. Brush the almond paste with a little boiled water then lift the sugarpaste over the cake and smooth down over top and sides. Trim away the edges and place on a 25 cm/ 10 inch board or serving plate.

Roll the white trimmings into a long strip and press round to cover the cake board then pinch the icing together with your thumb and finger or a scalloped modelling tool to make small ridges.

Colour 75 g/3 oz sugarpaste green and 15 g/¹/₂ oz red. Roll out the green paste thinly and cut out 3 large holly leaves with a cutter or follow the pattern on page 249. Mark veins onto the leaves with a sharp knife. Roll 24 small balls from the remaining green sugarpaste and place these round the base of the cake.

Dampen underneath each leaf lightly with a little cold boiled water then position the 3 leaves in the centre of the cake. Model the red sugarpaste into red berries and place these in the centre of the leaves.

Poinsettia Chocolate Cake

Serves 12–14

For the cake base:

1 x 20 cm/8 inch round chocolate
cake (*see* page 29),
covered in almond paste
(*see* page 56)

To decorate:

1 batch chocolate covering icing
(*see* page 50)
icing sugar, for dusting
350 g/12 oz ready-to-roll
sugarpaste icing
green, rust, red and yellow paste
food colouring

Knead the chocolate icing until soft then roll out on a surface lightly dusted with icing sugar to a circle large enough to cover the cake. Lift onto the cake and smooth down over the top and sides, then trim the edges neatly.

Colour the sugarpaste in 75 g/3 oz batches in green, rust, red and orange. Roll out the green sugarpaste thinly on a surface lightly dusted with icing sugar and stamp out 4 large holly leaves using a cutter or the pattern on page 249. Mark on veins with a sharp knife.

Roll out the rust coloured sugarpaste thinly and stamp out 10 flower petals using a flower cutter. Roll the red sugarpaste into small balls then repeat with the yellow sugarpaste and the green and rust trimmings.

Place the 4 green holly leaves in the centre of the cake and position the rust flower petals on top of these overlapping them as shown. Place 4 small yellow balls in the centre of the flower. Scatter 10 small red balls round the flower and lightly press onto the chocolate icing. Make a colourful border with the remaining small balls, placing them alternately round the base of the cake to trim.

Hogmanay Party Cupcakes

Makes 12

For the cakes:

1 batch vanilla cupcakes
(*see* page 32)

To decorate:

1 batch buttercream (*see* page 38)
450 g/1 lb ready-to-roll
sugarpaste icing
yellow, green and lilac paste
food colourings
icing sugar, for dusting

Trim the tops of the cakes flat if they have peaked slightly. Lightly coat the top of each cake with a little buttercream.

Colour half the sugarpaste a pale cream shade and roll out thinly on a surface lightly dusted with icing sugar. Stamp out circles 6 cm/2½ inches wide (*see* page 251) and place these on the buttercream to cover the top of each cupcake.

Colour the remaining icing green and lilac. Mould the green icing into stems as pictured or, to be more thistle-like, place a small ball onto each thin stem to form the bulbous part. Mark the bulbous parts of the stems with 'spikes', and position on the fairy cakes.

Roll out the lilac sugarpaste into a long thin strip about 2.5 cm/ 1 inch wide. Cut with a knife, or snip with scissors, three quarters of the way through the paste, then roll up to form a tassel for a thistle top and attach to the top of a stem. Repeat with the remaining cakes.

Aquamarine Engagement Cake

Serves 40

For the cake base:

1 x 20 cm/8 inch round Madeira
cake (*see* page 30),
covered in almond paste
(*see* page 56)
1 x 15 cm/6 inch round Madeira
cake, covered in almond glaze

To decorate:

1.75 kg/3¹/₂ lb ready-to-roll
sugarpaste icing
turquoise paste food colouring
icing sugar, for dusting

Cut off 450 g/1 lb sugarpaste and set aside. Colour the remaining sugarpaste pale turquoise with a few spots of paste food colouring. Divide the sugarpaste into 750 g/1¹/₂ lb and 450 g/1 lb batches. Cover the larger cake with 750 g/1¹/₂ lb sugarpaste. Trim away the edges then repeat to cover the smaller cake.

Place the large cake on a 30 cm/12 inch cake drum and the smaller one on a 15 cm/6 inch thin round cake board. Push 4 sticks of thin wooden or plastic dowelling, cut to the depth of the cake into the base of the large cake. Stack the cakes.

Mould white roses with the reserved white sugarpaste (*see* page 62) and place in empty egg boxes lined with crumpled foil. Cut out small white leaves and mark on veins with a sharp knife.

Leave the roses and leaves to harden for 24 hours then dampen the underside of each with a little cold boiled water and position on top of the cake and between the tiers as shown.

Hearts Engagement Cake

Serves 12–16

For the cake base:

1 x 23 cm/9 inch square chocolate
cake (*see* page 29)

To decorate:

1 batch buttercream (*see* page 38)
1 kg/2^1/$_4$ lb ready-to-roll
sugarpaste icing
icing sugar, for dusting
brown paste food colouring

Trim the top of the cake flat if it has peaked. Cut the cake in half horizontally and spread one half with a little buttercream. Place the other layer on top and spread the remaining buttercream over the top and sides of the cake.

Cover the cake with 875 g/1^3/$_4$ lb sugarpaste, trim the edges, then place on a 30 cm/12 inch cake board. Colour the remaining sugarpaste in two batches one light brown and one dark brown.

Roll out one quarter of each batch thickly and stamp out a large heart shape in each colour, or follow the pattern on page 248. Leave the large hearts to firm on a sheet of nonstick baking parchment for 24 hours.

Roll out the remaining sugarpaste thinly and stamp out 15 dark and 15 light brown hearts. Dampen the underside of each heart with a little cold boiled water and stick on the top and sides of the cake in pairs of light and dark brown.

Make two small indentations in the white icing and stand the large hearts upright in them as shown. Finish by trimming with a length of silver ribbon round the base.

Lacework Wedding Cake

Serves 60–70

For the cake base:

1 x 20 cm/8 inch round rich fruit
cake (*see* page 26),
covered in almond paste
(*see* page 56)
1 x 15 cm/6 inch round rich fruit
cake, covered in almond paste

To decorate:

1.24 kg/2 lb 4 oz ready-to-roll
sugarpaste icing
peach and pale green paste
food colouring
icing sugar, for dusting
3 batches royal icing (*see* page 46)

Place the large cake on a 30 cm/12 inch round cake drum.
Place the small cake on a thin 15 cm/6 inch round board.

Colour 350 g/12 oz sugarpaste peach and 350 g/12 oz pale
green. Take balls of peach icing and model into petal shapes then
roll around a centre to make roses (*see* page 62). Make 8 peach
roses and leave them to harden for 3 hours in empty egg boxes
lined with crumpled foil. Repeat with 350 g/12 oz white sugarpaste
to make 8 white roses. Roll out the green icing on a surface lightly
dusted with icing sugar and stamp out 40 small green leaves and
buds. Leave to dry out for 3 hours on nonstick baking parchment.

Coat each cake with royal icing (*see* pages 57–58). Stack the
cakes on top of each other, using dowelling (*see* page 58). Fill a
piping bag fitted with a medium plain nozzle with royal icing and
pipe dots round the base of each cake to make a border. Pipe 'S'
shaped swirls and squiggles in a haphazard pattern on the top
and sides of the cake as shown.

Mould white sugarpaste trimmings into a pyramid shape and stick
the peach and white roses onto this as shown, filling in the gaps
with small green leaves and buds. Arrange the remaining roses
and leaves on the cake as shown.

Chocolate Wedding Cake

Serves 80

For the cake base:

1 x 25 cm/10 inch round chocolate
cake (*see* page 29), covered with
almond paste (*see* page 56)
1 x 20 cm/8 inch round chocolate
cake, covered with almond paste
1 x 15 cm/6 inch round chocolate
cake, covered with almond paste

To decorate:

4 batches chocolate covering icing
(*see* page 50)
1¹/₂ batches royal icing
(*see* page 46)
dark brown paste food colouring

Divide the chocolate covering into 1 kg/2 lb, 750 g/1¹/₂ lb and 450 g/1 lb batches. Knead the largest batch until soft then roll out to a circle large enough to cover the top and sides of the 25 cm/10 inch cake. Smooth down over the top and sides and flatten with an icing tool or the palms of your hands. Gather up the trimmings and repeat to cover the medium and small cakes. Place the large cake on a 40 cm/14 inch round cake drum. Place the medium cake on a thin 20 cm/8 inch round board and the small cake on a thin 15 cm/6 inch cake board.

Push 4 sticks of wooden or plastic dowelling evenly into the large cake base, cut to the depth of the cake. Repeat with the medium cake. Stack the cakes on top of each other.

Colour half the royal icing light brown, place in a piping bag fitted with a star nozzle then pipe a rope border evenly round the base of each cake. Colour the remaining icing in two batches one medium and one dark brown. Place the icing in three small piping bags fitted with small plain nozzles, one light, one medium and one dark brown. Following the design in the photo, pipe swirls and dots onto the sides of the cake in the 3 chocolate tones. Leave the icing to set for 5 hours before serving.

Silver Wedding Cake

Serves 80–100

For the cake base:

1 x 25 cm/10 inch round rich fuit
cake (*see* page 26),
covered with almond paste
(*see* page 56)
1 x 20 cm/8 inch round rich fruit
cake, covered with almond paste
1 x 15 cm/6 inch round rich fruit
cake, covered with almond paste

To decorate:

2.25 kg/4¹/₂ lb ready-to-roll
sugarpaste icing
icing sugar, for dusting
3 batches royal icing (*see* page 46)
edible silver balls

Divide the sugarpaste into 1 kg/2 lb, 750 g/1¹/₂ lb and 500 g/
1 lb 2 oz batches. Cover the largest cake with the largest batch.
Repeat to cover the medium and small cakes.

Place the large cake on a 40 cm/14 inch round cake drum. Place
the medium cake on a thin 20 cm/8 inch round board and the
small cake on a thin 15 cm/6 inch cake board. Stack the cakes
on top of each other using dowelling (*see* page 58).

Place one quarter of the royal icing in a piping bag fitted with a
small plain nozzle. Pipe a border of small dots round the base of
the large cake, then repeat with the medium and small cakes.
Mark the flower shapes as a guide onto the sides of the cake
with a small skewer. Fill a bag fitted with a small plain nozzle with
royal icing. Pipe the outline of the petals round the guide then
take a fine paintbrush and dampen the tip with a little cold boiled
water. Use the brush to pull the icing from the outside into the
middle of the flower. Place a small silver ball in the centre of each
flower. Pipe leaves and squiggles in a random pattern onto the
sides of the cake to represent lace work. Stick silver balls onto
the cake at intervals. Repeat with the top two tiers and leave the
icing to dry out for 5 hours.

Golden Wedding Bells Cake

Serves 20

For the cake base:

1 x 20 cm/8 inch round rich fruit
cake (*see* page 26),
covered with almond paste
(*see* page 56)

To decorate:

1.25 kg/2¼ lb ready-to-roll
sugarpaste icing
icing sugar, for dusting
edible gold dusting powder
granulated sugar
1 small gold candle (optional)

Weigh 550 g/1¼ lb sugarpaste and roll out on a surface lightly dusted with icing sugar to a circle large enough to cover the top and sides of the cake. Brush the almond paste with a little cold boiled water then lift the sugarpaste over the cake and smooth down over the top and sides. Trim away the edges and place on a 25 cm/10 inch board or serving plate. Roll the white trimmings into a long strip and press round the base to cover the cake board.

Roll out a thin sausage of sugarpaste about 20 cm/8 inches. Place on top of the cake, mould round into the shape of a bell and press the ends together to neaten. Shape another bell then place centrally on the cake.

Make a loop shape on top of each bell then roll 2 small balls and position under each bell. Roll the remaining sugarpaste into small balls then place these round the base of the cake to make a neat border.

Just before serving mix a little gold dusting powder with 2 tsp granulated sugar. Carefully scatter the gold coloured sugar inside the outline of each bell. Press a small gold candle between the bells to finish, if liked.

Booties Christening Cake

Serves 20

For the cake base:

1 x 20 cm/8 inch round rich fruit
cake (*see* page 26),
covered in almond paste
(*see* page 56)

To decorate:

900 g/2 lb ready-to-roll
sugarpaste icing
blue paste food colouring
icing sugar, for dusting

Weigh 500 g/1¹/₄ lb sugarpaste and colour light blue with a few spots of paste food colouring. Roll out the blue sugarpaste on a surface lightly dusted with icing sugar to a circle large enough to cover the top and sides of the cake. Brush a little cold boiled water over the almond paste then lift the sugarpaste over the cake and smooth down over the top and sides. Trim the edges and place on a 25 cm/10 inch board or serving plate.

Colour a 15 g/¹/₂ oz scrap of blue icing a darker shade and model into a tiny pair of shoes. Model 75 g/3 oz white sugarpaste into two oblongs, then fold over at one end to make a pair of booties. Flute out the tops into frills and trim each one with fine blue ribbon bow.

Roll out the remaining white icing thinly and stamp out letters for the baby's initials and decorative patterns. Brush the underside of each lightly with a little cold boiled water and press onto the cake.

Stick the large and small booties in place with a little cold boiled water then tie a length of blue gingham ribbon round the base, finishing with a bow to trim.

Pink Cradle Christening Cake

Serves 12–14

For the cake base:

1 x 20 cm/8 inch round Madeira
cake (*see* page 30),
covered in almond paste
(*see* page 56)

To decorate:

1.25 kg/2¹/₂ lb ready-to-roll
sugarpaste icing
icing sugar, for dusting
pink paste food colouring
small tube white piping icing
edible gold coated balls

Cover the cake with 550 g/1¹/₄ lb sugarpaste. Trim the edges and place on a 25 cm/10 inch board or serving plate. Roll the white trimmings into a ball and set aside. Colour 350 g/12 oz sugarpaste pink. Make the frills; roll out the sugarpaste and stamp out a fluted circle 6 cm/2¹/₂ inches wide with a pastry cutter. Cut away a small plain disc 3 cm/1¹/₄ inches wide from the centre and discard. Take a cocktail stick and roll back and forth until the sugarpaste begins to frill up *(see* page 64). Attach a section of frilled edge to the base of the cake, dampening with a little cold boiled water. Make more frilled sections to go right round the base of the cake.

For the crib, mould an oblong shape with white trimmings. Make a layer of white frills, as above and attach these to the base. Make a layer of pink frills and stick on top of the white ones, then add another layer of white frills. Shape a white piece of sugarpaste into a half moon shape, hollow out and stick on top of the frills at one end. Make a pink frilled edge and attach this round the dome shape. Model some pink sugarpaste into 2 thin sheets and place inside the crib. Pipe a border of small white dots around the crib and over the dome. Roll out the remaining pink sugarpaste thinly, stamp out small daisies, dampen and place on the pink border, then place a gold ball in each daisy to finish.

Easter Bunny Cupcakes

Makes 12

For the cakes:

1 batch vanilla cupcakes
(*see* page 32)

To decorate:

1 batch cream cheese frosting
(*see* page 44)
700 g/1^1/$_2$ lb ready-to-roll
sugarpaste icing
brown, green, yellow, pink and
black paste food colouring
^{1}/$_2$ batch royal icing (*see* page 46)

Place the cream cheese frosting in a piping bag fitted with a star nozzle and pipe a large swirl on top of each cake.

To make the rabbits, colour 350 g/12 oz sugarpaste brown, 175 g/6 oz pale green, 75 g/3 oz yellow and 15 g/^{1}/$_2$ oz pink. Roll a small ball of green sugarpaste for the body. Using brown sugarpaste, roll a small pear shape and flatten out for the head. Model 2 ears and stick to the back of the head with a little cold boiled water. Roll 2 small sausages for the arms and flatten out 2 ovals for the paws.

Decorate the face by modelling a scrap of white sugarpaste as shown, then stick to the face with a little cold boiled water. Make a small pink button nose and paint on 2 eyes with dots of black food colouring. Position the body, arms and paws in the frosting on the cake. Stick the head in place with a little cold boiled water.

Colour the royal icing a pale cream colour with a tiny spot of yellow colouring paste. Place the icing in a piping bag fitted with a small plain nozzle and pipe decorations on the ears and body as shown. Leave to dry for 1 hour.

Spring Daisy Cake

Serves 80–100

For the cake base:

1 x 25 cm/10 inch round rich
fruit cake (*see* page 27)
1 x 20 cm/8 inch round rich
fruit cake (*see* page 26)
1 x 15 cm/6 inch round rich
fruit cake

To decorate:

2.25 kg/4¹/₂ lb ready-to-roll
sugarpaste icing
lemon and green paste
food colourings
icing sugar, for dusting
1 batch royal icing (*see* page 46)
450 g/1 lb bought flower paste
cornflour, for dusting

Colour the sugarpaste pale lemon. Cover the largest cake with 1 kg/2 lb icing; the medium cake with 750 g/1¹/₂ lb icing and the small cake with 450 g/1 lb icing. Place the large cake on a 40 cm/14 inch round cake drum, the medium cake on a thin 20 cm/8 inch round board and the small cake on a thin 15 cm/6 inch cake board. Using dowelling (*see* page 58), stack the cakes.

Colour the royal icing pale yellow and place in a piping bag fitted with a medium plain nozzle. Pipe a rope border round the base of each cake and leave to dry for 24 hours. Reserve the remaining royal icing.

Colour a third of the flower paste greenish yellow for the centres. Roll out the white flower paste very thinly on a surface dusted with cornflour. Using a fine large cutter, stamp out a daisy shape, then flute this up to flick out the petals. Place in a piece of crumpled foil then make another layer. Dampen the first layer and press the petals on top of this. Roll a tiny ball of green paste, flatten out then mark with a skewer to make the centre of the daisy. Press onto the petals and leave to dry out for 24 hours. Make 30 large and 30 small daisies. When firm stick to the top and sides of the cakes with the remaining royal icing.

Spring Daffodil Cupcakes

Makes 12

For the cakes:

1 batch vanilla cupcakes
(*see* page 32)

To decorate:

1 batch buttercream (*see* page 38)
450 g/1 lb ready-to-roll
sugarpaste icing
green, yellow and orange paste
food colouring
icing sugar, for dusting

Trim the tops of the cakes flat if they have peaked slightly. Lightly coat the top of each with a little buttercream.

Colour half the sugarpaste light green and roll out thinly on a surface lightly dusted with icing sugar. Stamp out circles 6 cm/2^{1}/$_{2}$ inches wide, or use the template on page 251 and place these on the buttercream to cover the top of each cupcake.

Colour three quarters of the remaining icing yellow and a quarter orange. Roll out the yellow icing on some baking parchment and mark out thin petal shapes.

Take 6 petals and pinch each one together. Place these onto the green icing in a circle, then mould a piece of orange icing into a pea-sized ball. Mould this into a cone shape, flatten slightly, and place in the centre of the flower.

Harvest Festival Cupcakes

Makes 12

For the cakes:

1 batch vanilla cupcakes
(*see* page 32)

To decorate:

1 batch cream cheese frosting
(*see* page 44)
pale green orange, red, green,
brown paste food colourings
225 g/8 oz ready-to-roll
sugarpaste icing

Colour the frosting pale green and smooth over the top of each cupcake.

Colour the sugarpaste in small batches of orange, red, green and brown.

Model the green paste into cabbages by making tiny leaves and wrapping round each other.

Make carrots by rolling orange paste into tiny cones, press green sugarpaste through a garlic press to make carrot leaves.

Make potatoes by rolling cream paste into irregular shaped balls.

Make tomatoes by rolling red paste into small red balls and top each one with a green leaf trim. Place a different vegetable on top of each cupcake.

Entwined Valentine's Cake

❦

Serves 12–14

For the cake base:

1 x 20 cm/8 inch round Madeira
cake (*see* page 30)

To decorate:

¹/₂ batch buttercream (*see* page 38)
700 g/1¹/₂ lb ready-to-roll
sugarpaste icing
icing sugar, for dusting
red and pink paste food colouring

Trim the top of the cake flat if it has peaked and cut the cake
in half horizontally. Spread one half with one quarter of the
buttercream, replace the top layer then spread the remaining
buttercream thinly over the top and sides of the cake.

Cover the cake with 550 g/1¹/₄ lb white sugarpaste. Trim away
the edges then place the cake on a doily on a 25 cm/10 inch
cake board or flat serving plate.

Colour half the remaining sugarpaste red and the other half
pink. Roll out the pastes thinly and cut out 2 large heart shapes
with a cutter or follow the pattern on page 248. Dampen the
underside of the red heart with a little cold boiled water and
stick this onto the top of the cake.

Repeat with the pink heart and stick this onto the cake
overlapping the red one. Stamp out 8 tiny flowers from pink
scraps. Stick equally round the top of the cake as shown. Finish
the cake by trimming with a pink satin ribbon.

Halloween Pumpkin Cake

Serves 12–14

For the cake base:

1 x 20 cm/8 inch round chocolate cake (*see* page 29)

To decorate:

2 batches buttercream (*see* page 38)
orange, yellow, black and green paste food colouring

Trim the top of the cake flat if it has peaked then cut away a small half moon shape from the top and base to give the cake a slightly oval shape. Place the cake on a 30 cm/12 inch serving plate or cake board.

Colour two thirds of the buttercream bright orange. Colour half of the remaining buttercream yellow, then half black and half green. Place the black icing in a piping bag fitted with small star nozzle. Using the point of a sharp knife or a kitchen skewer, mark out the pattern of the face as shown, into the cake crust. Hold the bag directly over the cake and gently press out small stars round the outline with the black buttercream.

Fill a piping bag fitted with a small star nozzle with the yellow buttercream. Fill in the eyes, nose and mouth with small piped yellow stars, taking care to keep inside the black outline.

Fill a piping bag fitted with a small star nozzle with the orange buttercream. Pipe small stars all over the cake to fill in all the spaces. Fill a piping bag fitted with a small star nozzle with the green buttercream. Pipe a green stalk on top of the cake in stars to finish the cake.

Spooky Ghosts Cake

Serves 12–14

For the cake base:

1 x 20 cm/8 inch round chocolate
cake (*see* page 29)

To decorate:

1 batch buttercream (*see* page 38)
3 mini chocolate Swiss rolls
175 g/6 oz ready-to-roll
sugarpaste icing
icing sugar, for dusting
1 batch glacé icing (*see* page 54)
black paste food colouring

Trim the top of the cake flat if it has peaked. Cut the cake in half horizontally and spread one half with a little buttercream. Place the other half on top and sandwich the layers together. Place the cake on a 25 cm/10 inch flat serving plate or board. Place the remaining buttercream in a piping bag fitted with a large star nozzle.

Make the ghosts. Cut the Swiss rolls in half to make 6 pieces. Pipe a little buttercream on top of each cake. Divide the sugarpaste into six 25 g/ 1 oz balls then roll each one out to an 11 cm/4¼ inch circle on a surface lightly dusted with icing sugar. Press the outer edges of the circles between your fingertips to make them flute up. Lift each circle over a piece of cake and smooth over the top leaving the edges loosely draped.

Colour the glacé icing black with paste food colouring then quickly spread this over the top of the cake as it will start to set quickly. Place the ghosts in the wet icing, lifting the sugarpaste to form folds round them. Paint 2 black dots for eyes on each ghost with the tip of a fine brush. Leave the black icing to set for 30 minutes.

Using the reserved buttercream, pipe a straight line from the base to the top the cake, flicking away the bag as you finish to make a peak. Continue piping until the sides of the cake are coated with buttercream. Serve within 1 hour.

Children's

Cakes

Look no further than this chapter for the perfect cake design to delight your children, whether for a party or as a fun teatime treat. Try the Pirate Cupcakes, a fun snack for any child's playtime, or the Blue Guitar Cake, bound to inspire kids with musical aspirations. Alternatively, let your imagination run away with you with a stunning Under The Sea Cake complete with an octopus and starfish.

Busy Bees Cake

Serves 12–15

For the cake base:

1 x 23 cm/9 inch round Madeira cake (*see* page 30)

To decorate:

1 batch buttercream (*see* page 38)
1.3 kg/3 lb ready-to-roll sugarpaste icing
icing sugar, for dusting
green, orange, yellow, red and black paste food colourings
black floristry stamens

Trim the top of the cake. Cut in half horizontally and spread with one third of the buttercream, then sandwich back together. Spread buttercream round the top and sides of the cake. Cover the cake with 700 g/1½ lb sugarpaste and place on a 25 cm/10 inch cake board. Colour 125 g/4 oz sugarpaste pale green, 225 g/8 oz orange, 75 g/3 oz yellow, 75 g/3 oz rust, 25 g/1 oz red and 75 g/3 oz black. Roll out the green sugarpaste to a thin strip long enough to go round the base of the cake. Make a fluted edge and then stick round the cake. Roll out the sugarpastes thinly and with a flower cutter stamp out 8 large yellow daisies; 8 large white daisies; 3 large, 3 medium and 3 small orange daisies and 3 large, 3 medium and 3 small rust daisies. Roll yellow or orange scraps into tiny balls and make a centre in each flower. Leave the daisies to dry out on nonstick baking parchment.

For the bees, roll 5 orange scraps of paste into small ovals; wrap 2 thin bands of black paste round these. Flatten 2 small balls of white icing for the wings and press onto the bees. Paint on a face with a fine brush dipped in black food colour. Position 2 black stamens over the face. For the ladybirds, model 2 ovals from black paste. Flatten a ball of red icing, place on the oval then make a slit to form the wings. Decorate with black dots, make white eyes and mouth with thin scraps of white paste, then position stamens over the head. Dampen the underside of the daisies, bees and ladybirds and place on the cake.

Blue Guitar Cake

Serves 10–12

For the cake base:

1 x 20 cm/8 inch Madeira cake
(*see* page 30)
6 tbsp apricot glaze

To decorate:

900 g/2 lb ready-to-roll
sugarpaste icing
blue, yellow and pink paste
food colouring
icing sugar, for dusting
small tubes of blue and white
piping icing

Cut the cake in half horizontally and spread with 3 tbsp of apricot glaze. Sandwich the cake back together and spread the remaining glaze over the top and sides.

Colour 700 g/1½ lb of the sugarpaste a pale blue and use to cover the cake. Place the cake on a cake board or flat serving plate.

Colour 125 g/4 oz of the sugarpaste yellow then roll out thinly and cut into 15 stars using a cutter or the template on page 251. Dampen the underside of each star and stick onto the cake as shown.

Colour 75 g/3 oz sugarpaste a deeper blue and use to model the base and frame of a guitar. Colour 25 g/1 oz sugarpaste dark pink, shape into a small disc and place in the middle of the body of the guitar.

Dampen the underside of the guitar shape with a little cold boiled water then stick onto the cake. Snip a fine tip away from the icing tube and pipe fine lines of white icing to represent the strings. Pipe on musical notes with the blue icing.

Football Fun Cake

Serves 10–12

For the cake base:

1 bowl shaped Madeira cake
baked in a 2 litre/4 pint
ovenproof bowl
(*see* pages 30–31)

To decorate:

1 batch chocolate buttercream
(*see* page 38)
1 batch vanilla buttercream
(*see* page 38)

Trim the top of the cake if it has peaked, turn it upside down then trim the crust from the cake to make a neat rounded shape. Place on a cake board or flat serving plate.

Make a hexagon template by cutting an 8 cm/3 inch round from greaseproof paper. Fold the round in half then fold the half into three. Cut a straight line between the ends of the fold lines then open out to make a hexagon shape.

Place the chocolate buttercream in a piping bag fitted with a star nozzle. Using the template as a guide, mark the cake crust with a sharp knife to outline the hexagon shapes. Pipe round the outline in small stars, then fill in alternate hexagons with piped chocolate stars.

Clean the bag and nozzle and fill with vanilla buttercream. Pipe small stars into the remaining hexagon shapes.

Pirate Cupcakes

Makes 12

For the cakes:

1 batch vanilla cupcakes
(*see* page 32)

To decorate:

1 batch buttercream
(*see* page 38)
450 g/1 lb ready-to-roll
sugarpaste icing
pink, blue, yellow and black paste
food colouring
icing sugar, for dusting
edible coloured balls and
small sweets
small tube red gel icing

Lightly coat the top of each cupcake with buttercream.

Colour the sugarpaste pale pink and roll out thinly on a surface dusted with icing sugar. Stamp out circles 6 cm/2^1/$_2$ inches wide and place these on the buttercream on top of each cupcake.

Colour some scraps of sugarpaste blue, some yellow and a small amount black. Make triangular shapes from the blue and yellow icing and place these onto the pink icing at an angle to form hats.

Stick coloured edible balls into the icing to decorate the hats. Make thin sausages from the black icing and press these across the cupcakes, then make tiny eye patches from black icing. Stick on a tiny sweet for each eye and pipe on red mouths with the gel icing.

Pretty Pink Party Cake

Serves 10–12

For the cake base:

1 x 20 cm/8 inch round Madeira
cake (*see* page 30)
6 tbsp apricot glaze

To decorate:

1.125 kg/2¼ lb ready-to-roll
sugarpaste icing
icing sugar, for dusting
pink paste food colouring

Cut the cake in half horizontally and spread with 3 tbsp apricot glaze. Sandwich the cake back together and spread the remaining glaze over the top and sides.

Cover the cake with 550 g/1½ lb of the sugarpaste. Trim away the excess icing round the base and gather up the scraps.

Add the scraps to the remaining icing and colour half of this pale pink and half a deeper shade of pink, adding a little more paste colour. Roll out one quarter of the light pink icing very thinly and cut out 12 large and 12 small flowers shapes using a stamper or cutting round the templates on page 253. Repeat with the darker pink icing.

Roll the remaining icing into 15 small light pink round balls and 15 dark pink balls. Place the cake on a 23 cm/10 inch round cake board and position the balls round the base, pressing lightly into the cake.

Dampen the back of the large and small daisies with a little cold boiled water and stick onto the cake in an alternating pattern.

Ladybird Cake

Serves 30

For the cake base:

1 x 20 cm/8 inch round Madeira
cake (*see* page 30)
1 x 15 cm/6 inch round
Madeira cake

To decorate:

1½ batches buttercream
(*see* page 38)
1.8 kg/4 lb ready-to-roll
sugarpaste icing
green, yelow, red, black and pink
paste food colouring
icing sugar, for dusting
1 bought chocolate
marshmallow biscuit
small tube of black piping icing

Cut the tops of both cakes level. Cut each cake in half, spread 1 half with buttercream, sandwich back together. Spread buttercream thinly over the top and sides of the cakes. Cover the larger cake with 700 g/1½ lb green sugarpaste; the smaller with 450 g/1 lb. Place the small cake on a 15 cm/6 inch cake board. Stack the cakes. Colour the scraps, plus 50 g/2 oz sugarpaste dark green and roll out thinly. Cut out 30 leaf shapes and mark veins on these with a sharp knife. Using cold boiled water, stick 8 leaves on top of the small cake then stick leaves on the sides of both cakes. Roll 75 g/3 oz yellow icing into 30 tiny balls and place as shown. Roll out 50 g/2 oz white icing and stamp out 14 white flowers. Using scraps of yellow icing make small dots for the centres. Stick the flowers onto the sides of the cake.

Colour 275 g/10 oz sugarpaste red. Roll out one quarter thinly and use to cover the biscuit. Make 8 small balls, flatten into ovals and place on toothpicks. Press into the small cake round the base. Roll 16 small red balls, flatten into ovals and stick onto the sides of the cakes. Colour 50 g/2 oz icing black and roll half into a ball for the head. Roll thin sausages to make curly feelers and leave to dry and harden. Cut out 8 small dots and place on the red oblong, adding a strip of black to divide the back into 2 wings. Place the head and body on top of the green leaves on the top cake. Make eyes and a mouth with white icing, then add tiny balls of pink paste for the cheeks. Decorate the small ladybirds with small dots of piped black icing. Position the feelers on the ladybird's head when they are hard.

Nelly The Elephant Cake

Serves 14–16

For the cake base:

1 x 20 cm/8 inch round Madeira cake (*see* page 30)
1 x 15 cm/6 inch round Madeira cake

To decorate:

2 batches buttercream (*see* page 38)
green, red, yellow, blue, orange and black paste food colouring
1.25 kg/2¼ lb ready-to-roll sugarpaste icing
icing sugar, for dusting

Cut the tops of both cakes level if they have peaked then cut each cake in half and spread one half with a little buttercream. Sandwich the cakes back together. Colour the remaining buttercream lime green and spread thickly over the top and sides of the cakes. Place the smaller cake on a thin 15 cm/6 inch round cake board and place on top of the larger one.

Colour the sugarpaste in 175 g/6 oz batches in red, yellow, pale green, blue, and orange and 50 g/2 oz grey. Roll out the colours, excluding the grey, thinly then cut wide and narrow strips. Trim and stick to the sides of the larger cake. Roll tiny balls from the remaining icing and place these around the base of the large and the small cake in alternating colours. Cut out small and larger discs using a cutter or a clean bottle cap, then press on to the decorate the top cake as shown. Roll a red scrap into a thin sausage twirl then press onto the cake as shown.

Mould the grey icing into an elephant. Make a large ball for the body and a smaller ball for the head. Flatten these slightly and press together. Make 4 thick sausages for the legs then press to the body as shown. Flatten out 2 small balls to make ears and press onto the head, then make a sausage shaped trunk and press onto the head. Make a small red hat with a yellow ball and place on top of the elephant's head. Roll 2 scraps of white icing into tiny discs for the eyes and place a tiny dot of black paste in each one.

Naughty Mice Cake

Serves 10–12

For the cake base:

1 bowl shaped Madeira cake
baked in a 2 litre/4 pint
ovenproof bowl
(*see* pages 30–31)

To decorate:

1 batch of vanilla flavoured
buttercream (*see* page 38)
1.125 kg/2^1/$_4$ lb ready-to-roll
sugarpaste icing
yellow, pink and black paste
food colourings
icing sugar, for dusting

Trim the top of the cake flat if it has peaked and turn the cake upside down. Cut the cake in half horizontally and spread with one third of the buttercream. Sandwich the cakes together then spread the remaining buttercream over the top and sides of the cake in a thin layer.

Colour 900 g/2 lb of the sugarpaste pale yellow and use to cover the cake. Trim the excess round the base of the cake and keep the scraps. Place the cake on a 30 cm/12 in round cake board or flat plate.

Colour 25 g/1 oz sugarpaste scraps a darker yellow. Cut out 6 small discs 2 cm/^{3}/$_4$ inches with the wide end of an icing nozzle. Press the discs around the cake into the pale yellow icing. Use 125 g/4 oz white icing to model the mice. Using 15 g/^{1}/$_2$ oz, model a teardrop shaped head, turning the point upwards. Make 3 more heads then flatten 8 tiny balls into ears for each mouse. Colour white scraps pale pink and roll into 4 tiny balls for the noses.

Model the remaining white scraps into back legs and a tail. Moisten the underneath of each head and tail with a little cold boiled water and position around the cake. Stick on the ears and noses and paint on the eyes with a tiny dab on black food paste using the tip of a fine paintbrush.

Hungry Bunny Cake

Serves 10–12

For the cake base:

1 x 20 cm/8 inch round Madeira
cake (*see* page 30)
6 tbsp apricot glaze

To decorate:

1.30 kg/2 lb 10 oz ready-to-roll
sugarpaste icing
icing sugar, for dusting
green, orange and blue
paste food colourings

Cut the top of the cake level and spread the cake with apricot glaze. Cover the cake with 550 g/1¼ lb sugarpaste. Roll out 125 g/4 oz white sugarpaste thinly and use to cover a 25 cm/10 inch cake board. Trim the edges then place the cake onto the covered board. Colour 225 g/8 oz icing green, 75 g/3 oz orange and 75 g/3 oz bright blue. Roll the green icing into long thin strips and coil these round in small spiral shapes. Press the spirals all around the base of the cake to form a border. Roll the orange sugarpaste into small cones to represent carrots and mark ridges on each one with the point of a knife. Flatten out some green icing to make carrot tops and cut the ends of these into a feathery shape with a knife tip.

Make the rabbit. Use a little cold boiled water to stick the pieces together. Model a small blue round for the head, 2 long flat ears, 2 sausages for the arms and a pear shape for the body. Stick the pear shape on the cake. Model 2 white feet and stick these either side of the pear shape. Stick a thin flat white oval onto the rabbit's front. Stick a white half circle onto the lower half of the head. Secure the head on the body with a small toothpick. Stick thin white strips onto the ears, then stick onto the head, bending the tips over. Make a tiny blue button nose and stick this onto the face. Stick the arms in place and flatten out the ends to make paws. Place a carrot in the rabbit's lap. Mark eyes on the face with a toothpick. Scatter the carrots on the cake.

First Birthday Cake

Serves 12–16

For the cake base:

1 x 20 cm/8 inch round Madeira
cake (*see* page 30)
1 x 15 cm/6 inch round
Madeira cake

To decorate:

1½ batches buttercream
(*see* page 38)
1.3 kg/3 lb ready-to-roll
sugarpaste icing
icing sugar, for dusting
pink and green paste
food colouring

Cut the tops of both cakes level if they have peaked, then cut each cake in half and spread one half with a little buttercream. Sandwich the cakes back together then spread the remaining buttercream thinly over the top and sides of the cakes. Place the large cake on a 25 cm/10 in round cake board. Place the smaller cake on a thin 15 cm/6 inch round cake board.

Cover the larger cake with 700 g/1½ lb sugarpaste. Cover the smaller cake with 450 g/1 lb sugarpaste. Stack the small cake on top of the larger one.

Colour the scraps and 225 g/8 oz sugarpaste in three batches: pale pink, deeper pink, pale green. Roll out thinly and cut wide and narrow strips in all three colours then trim and stick to the sides of the larger cake with a little cold boiled water.

Cut out small and large discs using a cutter or a clean bottle cap, then press on to decorate the top cake as shown. Mould scraps of green icing into a sausage and mould into a '1' for the centre of the cake. Make butterflies (*see* page 63) from pink scraps, leave to dry and attach with a little cold boiled water. Trim the cake with a thin satin ribbon.

Racing Cars Cake

Serves 18

For the cake base:

1 x 23 cm/9 inch square Madeira cake (*see* page 30)

To decorate:

$^1/_2$ batch buttercream (*see* page 38)
$^1/_2$ shop-bought Swiss roll
1.125 kg/2$^1/_4$ lb ready-to-roll sugarpaste icing
icing sugar, for dusting
green, yellow, blue, lilac and black paste food colourings
240 cm/100 inches thin liquorice bootlace sweets
1 round and 3 square liquorice allsorts sweets
16 round dolly mixture sweets
3 candles and 1 chequered flag

Cut the top of the cake completely flat then spread with three quarters of the buttercream. Spread the remaining buttercream over the top and sides of the Swiss roll. Cover the cake with 750 g/1$^1/_2$ lb sugarpaste. Trim away the edges and collect up the scraps in a ball.

Colour 125 g/4 oz sugarpaste pale green and roll out into an oblong large enough to cover the Swiss roll. Press down over the Swiss roll to make a mound shape, trim the edges then place in the centre of the cake. Use the green trimmings to make grass by pressing through a garlic press or cutting finely. Scatter on the mound. Take a 102 cm/40 inch strip of liquorice and press round the base of the cake into the icing. Repeat with another strip to make a border round the top. Press a 38 cm/15 inch strip of liquorice round the grassy mound and then place short strips to mark the race track as shown.

Colour the remaining sugarpaste yellow, blue and lilac in 50 g/2 oz batches for the cars. Halve each batch and shape a square with one half. Shape the other half into an oblong and press together to make the car body. Position the car on the track and press on 4 sweets for wheels and 1 for a steering wheel. Place a square sweet for the seat and press in a candle next to this. Make 2 more cars then paint numbers on each with black food colouring. Place a round sweet in the grassy mound and place a flag into this.

Happy Chick Cake

Serves 10–12

For the cake base:

1 x 20 cm/8 inch round chocolate cake (*see* page 29)

To decorate:

8 tbsp chocolate nut spread, softened
1.25 kg/2¹/₂ lb ready-to-roll sugarpaste icing
green, orange, brown and yellow paste food colourings
icing sugar, for dusting
1 large round chocolate wafer biscuit 7.5 cm/3 inches wide

Cut the cake in half horizontally and spread one half with 3 tbsp chocolate nut spread. Smooth the remaining spread over the top and sides of the cake. Reserve 15 g/¹/₂ oz white icing and then colour 125 g/4 oz green, 25 g/1 oz bright orange, 15 g/¹/₂ oz brown and colour the remainder bright yellow. Cover a 25 cm/10 inch round cake board with the green sugarpaste, then trim the sides neatly. Place the cake on the board and cover with 700 g/1¹/₂ lb of the yellow icing, scalloping the edges and draping one longer edge of the icing to the right as shown.

Roll out one third of the remaining yellow sugarpaste to a circle large enough to cover the chocolate biscuit. Dab the biscuit with a little chocolate spread then press the yellow icing on and tuck the edges underneath. Mark ridges all around the disc with a fork. Model the remaining yellow sugarpaste into 2 wing shapes and mark with the tines of a fork to represent feathers. Mark 4 deep ridges on each wing then position the wings on the cake.

Model the orange sugarpaste into a diamond shape for the beak, raise the edges into a ridge and place on the round head shape. Roll out the white icing into 2 rounds and flatten out, then roll 2 smaller rounds in brown icing. Place the brown discs on the white discs and place a small white dot of icing on each eye. Place the eyes on the chick's head above the beak, the press the head onto the cake above the wings.

My Pink Handbag Cake

Serves 15

For the cake base:

1 x 20 cm/8 inch round chocolate
cake (*see* page 29)
5 bought chocolate cake
bars, 7 cm/2¹/₂ inches length

To decorate:

1¹/₄ batches chocolate buttercream
(*see* page 38)
1.25 kg/2¹/₂ lb ready-to-roll
sugarpaste icing
pink and black paste
food colourings
icing sugar, for dusting
3 white sugarpaste roses
(*see* page 62)

Trim the top from the cake flat and cut the cake in half horizontally. Reserve one quarter of the buttercream. Spread one cake half with buttercream, then place the other layer on top. Spread the top and sides of the cake thinly with buttercream. Colour 900 g/2 lb sugarpaste deep pink and 225 g/8 oz black. Cover the cake with 550 g/1¹/₄ lb of the pink sugarpaste, then place on a serving plate.

Place 2 cake bars side by side. Spread with a little buttercream and place another 2 on top. Spread again and place the last bar in the centre. Spread all over with buttercream to stick the pieces together. Roll out 275 g/10 oz pink sugarpaste to an oblong, 25 cm/10 inches x 20 cm/8 inches. Drape the pink paste over the cakes and smooth down over the top and sides. Tuck the edges underneath, then smooth with your hands until you make a handbag shape.

Roll the black sugarpaste into a sausage, then roll this to flatten to about 1 cm/¹/₂ inch width. Using a little boiled water, stick the black trim around the top, sides and flap of the bag. Model a handle and stick this on top of the bag. Place the bag on top of the cake and trim with stamped out daisies. Place 3 white sugarpaste roses next to the bag. Trim the base by rolling 25 black and 25 pink small balls of sugarpaste. Place these alternately round the base of the cake, pressing lightly onto the sides.

Fast Cars Cupcakes

Makes 12

For the cakes:

1 batch vanilla cupcakes
(*see* page 32)

To decorate:

225 g/8 oz ready-to-roll
sugarpaste icing
blue and red paste
food colourings
icing sugar, for dusting
350 g/12 oz fondant icing
sugar, sifted
6 tbsp royal icing sugar

Trim the tops of the cakes flat if they have peaked.

Colour half the sugarpaste blue and half red.

Roll each colour out thinly on a surface lightly dusted with icing sugar and cut out little car shapes, tracing round the pattern on page 249. Leave these for 2 hours to dry and harden.

Blend the fondant icing sugar with enough water to make an icing of a coating consistency. Spread over the top of each cupcake and, while still wet, place a car shape in the centre of each one.

Mix the royal icing sugar with enough water to make piping icing. Place in a small paper icing bag with the end snipped away. Pipe on wheels and windows and leave to dry for 30 minutes.

Daisy Chains Cake

Serves 18–20

For the cake base:

1 x 23 cm/9 inch round Madeira cake (*see* page 30)
1 x 15 cm/6 inch round Madeira cake

To decorate:

1 batch buttercream (*see* page 38)
2 kg/4 lb ready-to-roll sugarpaste icing
pale lemon, lilac, bright yellow, magenta, orange and green paste food colourings
icing sugar, for dusting
1 batch royal icing (*see* page 46)

Trim the tops of the cakes flat. Cut the larger cake in half horizontally and spread one half with a quarter of the buttercream. Replace the top layer and sandwich together. Spread the remaining buttercream thinly over the top and sides of both cakes. Colour 1.25 kg/2 lb sugarpaste pale lemon yellow. Cover the larger cake with 700 g/1½ lb yellow sugarpaste and place on a 30 cm/12 inch cake board; the smaller cake with 450 g/1 lb yellow sugarpaste and place on a thin 15 cm/6 inch cake board. Stack the cakes. Roll the trimmings into a ball. Colour the remaining sugarpaste in four batches of lilac, bright yellow, magenta and orange. Roll out each batch on a surface lightly dusted with icing sugar and stamp out 15 large and 10 small daisies in each colour, using a daisy cutter. Leave the daisies to dry out on a sheet of nonstick baking parchment for 2–3 hours to harden.

Place one third of the royal icing in a small piping bag with a plain nozzle and pipe a white dot in the centre of each flower. Stick the large and small daisies round the sides of the cake with a small dab of royal icing, alternating the colours. Take the ball of yellow trimmings and place in the centre of the small cake. Stick the remaining daisies round the ball to make a centrepiece. Colour the remaining royal icing green, place in a piping bag fitted with a star nozzle and pipe stars round each cake base to make a border. Fill a small piping bag fitted with a plain nozzle and pipe stalks and leaves round the daisy centrepiece.

Under The Sea Cake

Serves 14–16

For the cake base:

1 x 20 cm/8 inch round Madeira cake (*see* page 30)
1 x 15 cm/6 inch round Madeira cake

To decorate:

2 batches buttercream (*see* page 38)
blue, green, orange, pink, yellow, and black paste food colourings
700 g/1¹/₂ lb ready-to-roll sugarpaste icing

Cut the tops of both cakes level if they have peaked then cut each cake in half and spread one half with a little buttercream. Sandwich the cakes back together. Reserve 2 tbsp buttercream and colour the remaining bright blue. Spread thickly over the top and sides of both cakes. Place the large cake on a 30 cm/12 inch round cake board. Place the smaller cake on a thin 15 cm/6 inch round cake board, place on top of the larger one, then smooth round the join with a flat bladed knife. Dot blue buttercream alternately with the reserved white buttercream round the base of the board, add a few spots of extra blue colouring and swirl to make waves.

Colour 225 g/8 oz sugarpaste lime green, 50 g/2 oz orange, 125 g/4 oz bright pink and 175 g/6 oz yellow. Roll 50 g/2 oz lime green sugarpaste into a ball. Roll the remaining lime sugarpaste into 8 thin sausages, tapering the ends to a thin point. Place the 8 tentacles around the cake as shown, then place the octopus's head on top. Mould yellow sugarpaste into a small hat and bow tie and press in place. Cut out stars and seaweed with the remaining yellow paste and press around the board. Model a submarine with the orange sugarpaste paste and press in place on the smaller cake. Trim with a yellow scrap of sugarpaste and 2 white discs for portholes. Make 2 more white discs for the octopus's eyes and stick onto the head. Paint a tiny dot with black food colouring on each eye. Mould 16 small fishes with the pink sugarpaste and place 8 at the front and 8 at the back of the cake in a shoal.

Starburst Cake

Serves 10–12

For the cake base:

1 x 20 cm/8 inch round Madeira
cake (*see* page 30)
6 tbsp apricot glaze

To decorate:

1.125 kg/2¼ lb ready-to-roll
sugarpaste icing
icing sugar, for dusting
red, pale blue, pale green and
pink paste food colourings
¼ batch royal icing (*see* page 46)

Cut the cake in half horizontally and spread with 3 tbsp of the apricot glaze Sandwich the cake back together and spread the remaining glaze over the top and sides.

Cover the cake with 550g/1¼ lb of the sugarpaste. Trim away the excess icing round the base and gather up the scraps. Place the cake on a 25 cm/10 inch round cake board.

Divide the sugarpaste and trimmings into equal batches. Colour one batch red, one blue, one green and one pink. Roll out each batch of coloured sugarpaste thinly on a surface dusted lightly with icing sugar. Using a cutter or the templates on pages 250–51, cut out 5 large stars and 5 small stars in each colour and set aside.

Lightly dampen the underside of each star with a little cold boiled water and stick the stars onto the cake in a random pattern. Fill a piping bag fitted with a small star nozzle with royal icing and pipe a star border round the base.

Teddy Bear Cupcakes

Makes 12

For the cakes:

1 batch vanilla cupcakes
(*see* page 32)

To decorate:

225 g/8 oz ready-to-roll
sugarpaste icing
brown paste food colouring
325 g/11¹/₂ oz fondant
icing sugar, plus extra for dusting
6 tbsp royal icing sugar

Trim the tops of the cakes flat if they have peaked slightly.

Colour the sugarpaste brown. Dust a board with icing sugar. Roll the coloured sugarpaste thinly and stamp out bear shapes with a cutter or trace round the pattern on page 250 and mark on to the sugarpaste with a sharp knife. Leave to dry for 30 minutes.

Mix the fondant icing sugar with enough cold water to form a stiff shiny icing of coating consistency and colour this light brown. Flood the icing on top of each cupcake and, while still wet, place a bear shape onto this.

Mix the royal icing sugar with a little water to make a stiff paste and then pipe on eyes, a nose and buttons. Leave to set for 30 minutes.

Ice Cream Cones Cake

Serves 15–18

For the cake base:

1 x 23 cm/9 inch round Madeira cake (*see* page 30)
4 tbsp lemon curd

To decorate:

2 batches buttercream (*see* page 38)
8 ice cream cones
yellow, green, blue and pink paste food colourings
small brightly coloured sweets

Cut the sponge cake in half horizontally and spread one half with lemon curd. Sandwich the other layer on top and press together. Trim the top of the cake flat if it has peaked. Spread the top and sides of the cake with one batch of buttercream then place the cake on a 30 cm/12 inch cake board or flat serving plate.

Trim away one quarter of one side of each ice cream cone, from top to bottom so that they will sit flat against the cake. Press the cones into the side of the cake at regular intervals.

Colour half the buttercream bright yellow, then divide the remaining buttercream into three batches and colour these green, blue and pink. Place the yellow buttercream in a piping bag fitted with a large star nozzle and pipe a border round the base of the cake. Pipe the remaining yellow buttercream into two of the cones in a swirl.

Clean the piping bag and refill separately with each of the remaining batches of buttercream. Pipe swirls of different coloured buttercreams into the remaining cones. Scatter the outer edge of the cake with small coloured sweets just before serving.

Perky Penguins Cupcakes

Makes 12

For the cakes:

1 batch vanilla cupcakes
(*see* page 32)

To decorate:

$^{1}/_{4}$ batch buttercream
(*see* page 38)
900 g/2 lb ready-to-roll
sugarpaste icing
black and orange paste
food colourings
icing sugar, for dusting

Trim the top of each cake flat if they have peaked. Spread the top of each cake with a little buttercream. Colour 350 g/12 oz of the sugarpaste black and 75 g/3 oz orange. Roll out 450 g/1 lb white sugarpaste thinly on a surface lightly dusted with icing sugar. Cut out 12 circles 6 cm/2$^{1}/_{2}$ inches wide with a plain round cutter. Place a disc on top of each cupcake and press level.

Roll 10 g/$^{1}/_{4}$ oz black sugarpaste into a ball and flatten out one end. Roll a small sausage 6 cm/2$^{1}/_{2}$ inches long and drape it over the ball flicking up the ends to make 2 flippers. Roll a small black ball for the head. Roll out some white sugarpaste thinly and cut out a small teardrop shape. Stick the white shape onto the penguin's front with a little cold boiled water. Roll 2 small white balls for eyes and stick to the head.

Roll out the orange sugarpaste thickly and cut out 2 small rounds for the feet. Mark lines on with a skewer for the webbing, then place the feet on the cupcake. Dampen the base of the body and place on the feet. Dampen the head and place on the body. Make a small cone shape with orange sugarpaste and cut into this with a sharp knife to form a beak. Stick the beak onto the head, then finish the face by rolling 2 tiny black dots and sticking these onto the eyes.

Templates for Sugarpaste Shapes

LARGE HEART

MEDIUM HEART

EXTRA LARGE HEART

On these pages, you will find templates for some of the icing shapes as used in this book. Templates such as these are handy if you do not have a selection of metal cutters. Just trace the pattern you want onto a sheet of clear greaseproof paper or nonstick baking parchment. Roll out the sugarpaste thinly, then position the traced pattern over the icing. Mark over the pattern with the tip of a small sharp knife or a pin. Remove the paper and cut out the marked-on pattern with a small sharp knife. Voilà!

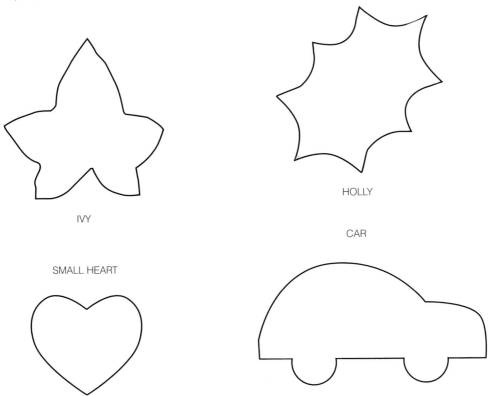

IVY

HOLLY

CAR

SMALL HEART

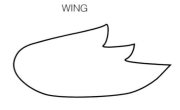

WING

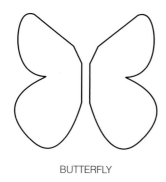

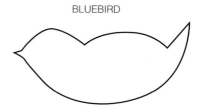

BLUEBIRD

BUTTERFLY

TEDDY BEAR

MEDIUM STAR

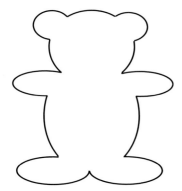

Templates for Sugarpaste Shapes 🍂 250

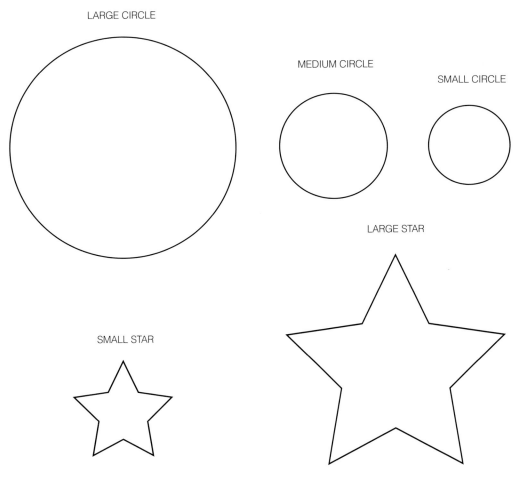

LARGE CIRCLE

MEDIUM CIRCLE

SMALL CIRCLE

LARGE STAR

SMALL STAR

Templates for Sugarpaste Shapes

LARGE STAR FLOWER

MEDIUM STAR FLOWER

SMALL STAR FLOWER

TINY DAISY

SMALL DAISY

FLOWER

SMALL FLOWER

PETAL & LARGE BUTTERFLY WING

 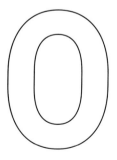

Templates for Sugarpaste Shapes

Index

Index